The Unintended Consequences of Killing Civilians

Table of Contents

Introduction...1

Media Influence..6

Political Implications..20

Complexity of Military Operations...31

Conclusion and Recommendations...43

Bibliography..50

Introduction

We are all, every citizen of the United States, morally complicit in the killing of innocents. Our elected representatives have given the executive branch of our government the right to kill as it sees fit. Each innocent killed rests on our conscience. There is

> no moral escape from our responsibility. To inflict pain without
> even understanding that pain is inflicted is one of the greatest of
> all moral failures. We no longer grasp how much we are hated in
> the world for our carelessness and insensitivity.[1]

Edward W. Wood, Jr., *Worshipping the Myths of World War II*

On January 13, 2004, Brigadier General Janis Karpinski, commander of the military prison at Abu Ghraib, near Baghdad, received an electronic mail message that would turn her world upside down. The command's Criminal Investigation Division was about to brief her boss, Lieutenant General Ricardo Sanchez, commander of Combined Joint Task Force Seven, on allegations of prisoner abuse in her facility. Apparently, the briefers had a collection of damning and disgusting photographs of prisoner abuse. This was the first she had heard of these allegations, and was not able to view the pictures until a week later, just before her meeting with General Sanchez on January 23. The pictures, taken by those who perpetuated the abuse, showed prisoners in all kinds of degrading poses. As a result, Sanchez admonished her for her inability to operate the prison. He fired all of her subordinate commanders and sent an expert team from U.S. Central Command to the prison to conduct remedial training on confinement operations, specifically the need to treat all detainees with dignity and respect. In April, when the CBS news program, *60 Minutes,* broadcast the story to the American public, Sanchez relieved Karpinski from command. The story of Abu Ghraib was, for the American public and the rest of the world, a reminder that some of the most shocking atrocities of war are those committed by the United States military.[2]

The abuses committed in the infamous cellblock 1A, such as beating prisoners unconscious, sodomizing a prisoner with a broom, stomping on prisoners' fingers, forced nudity and masturbation, and other forms of sexual humiliation, were not unique to Abu Ghraib. Similar abuses also occurred

---

[1] Edward W. Wood, Jr., *Worshipping the Myths of World War II: Reflections on America's Dedication to War* (Washington, D.C.: Potomac Books, Inc., 2006), 37.

[2] Janis Karpinski, *One Woman's Army: The Commanding General of Abu Ghraib Tells Her Story* (New York: Mirimax Books, 2005), 7-24.

at Guantanamo Bay, and in other facilities located in Iraq and Afghanistan since the start of the Global War on Terror.[3] An explanation for the widespread misconduct was twofold. First, there was political pressure placed on the military intelligence community (to gather more intelligence on the growing insurgencies), who then made recommendations to military prison cadre on deprivations which supposedly coaxed the prisoners into providing more information.[4] Second, according to a Presidential memo written February 7, 2002, members of Al-Qaeda and the Taliban were declared "unlawful combatants," and therefore "[did] not qualify as prisoners of war under Article [four] of Geneva."[5] The Bush administration stressed that [enhanced] "interrogation techniques" practiced at Guantanamo Bay and Abu Ghraib, and similar facilities not on American soil, did not fall under U.S. jurisdiction nor punishment under Geneva.[6] In other words, the detainees, *and* the U.S. soldiers responsible for them, were effectively operating from an ad hoc policy where neither clearly knew what to expect nor how to behave. Although the United States Supreme Court ruled on June 29, 2006 that government policies at Guantanamo Bay violated both the U.S. Code of Military Justice and the Geneva Conventions, and even though the United Nations called for the shutting down of the prison, it still remains operational today.[7]

The case of Abu Ghraib reveals the complexity of the operational environment, politically and tactically, within Iraq at the start of post-combat operations in 2004; however, this case sheds light on a larger problem, which is not new: the mistreatment of civilians[8] during violent conflicts. Mistreatment of civilians not party to a large-scale violent conflict is scalable and ranges from harassment to abuse/torture to murder, and sometimes occurs before an international military

---

[3] Ibid., 234-235; "Systemic Abuse of Afghan Prisoners," Human Rights Watch online (May 12, 2004), accessed February 21, 2012, http://www.hrw.org/news/2004/05/12/us-systemic-abuse-afghan-prisoners

[4] Karpinski, *One Woman's Army: The Commanding General of Abu Ghraib Tells Her Story,* 21.

[5] Craig R. Whitney, *The Abu-Ghraib Investigations: The Official Reports of the Independent Panel and the Pentagon on the Shocking Prisoner Abuse in Iraq,* Ed. Steven Strasser (New York: Public Affairs 2004), Appendix B, 176.

[6] Stjepan G. Mestrovic, *The Trials of Abu Ghraib: An Expert Witness Account of Shame and Honor* (Colorado: Paradigm Publishers, 2007), 26.

[7] Ibid., 195.

[8] Throughout this work, the word 'civilian' refers to indigenous personnel not party to the conflict.

intervention force enters the conflict. Consider the annihilation of the civilian population during the civil wars of the 1990s in Rwanda[9] and Bosnia.[10] In these "ethnopolitical" wars where disenfranchised groups forcefully came to power in a militaristic fashion, the opposing civilian population became the main target of genocide (or "ethnic cleansing").[11] Both conflicts resulted in over a million deaths and an equal amount of displaced personnel.[12] Though these internal civilian conflicts are the focus of humanitarian intervention debates of the day, another type of violence against civilians will be the focus of this work: that which is committed by the military intervention force.

The civilian casualties of the My Lai massacre during the Vietnam War numbered far less when compared with Rwanda and Bosnia, but the infamy of this incident is not how many were killed but by whom. The devastation inflicted upon the villagers was not the result of internal political strife. In March of 1968, a platoon of soldiers from the Americal Division killed 500 people (in four hours) in a village allegedly controlled by the enemy. Although there were no enemy personnel in My Lai, the mission was still carried out, which meant men, women, children, and animals were brutally killed, and the entire village was burned to the ground.[13] Also during the Vietnam War, in February of 1970, at Son Thang, U.S. Marines killed sixteen women and children when ordered to "shoot first, and ask questions later."[14] Examples presented in this paper of those fighting in current conflicts in the Middle East resemble the seemingly criminal behavior of service members characterized in the Vietnam War examples above. The perceived lack of empathy for civilians (historically and

---

[9] Joshua S. Goldstein, *Winning the War on War* (New York: Penguin Group, 2011), 78-87.

[10] Ibid., 87-91.

[11] Thomas G. Weiss, *Military-Civilian Interactions: Intervening in Humanitarian Crises* (New York: Oxford: Rowman and Littlefield Publishers, Inc., 1999), 21.

[12] Ibid.

[13] Jonathan Glover, *Humanity: A Moral History of the Twentieth Century* (New Haven: London: Yale University Press, 2000), 58-59. See also Seymour Hersh, *My Lai-4: A Report on the Massacre and its Aftermath* (New York: Vintage, 1970); Joseph Goldstein, Burke Marshall and Jack Schwartz, *The My Lai Massacre and Its Cover Up: Beyond the Reach of Law? The Peers Commission Report with a Supplement and Introductory Essay on the Limits of the Law* (New York: The Free Press, 1976).

[14] Stjepan G. Mestrovic, *Rules of Engagement? A Social Anatomy of American War Crime: Operation Iron Triangle, Iraq* (New York: Algora Publishing, 2008), 21; Quote from Gary D. Solis, *Son Thang: An American War Crime* (New York: Bantam, 1997), ix.

presently) points to ambiguities about who the enemy is, rules of engagement, as well as the ongoing debate about the nature of military intervention in internal conflicts. In addition, the civilian casualty examples of the current war in the Middle East emphasize changes that have occurred within the media, politics, and military operations since World War II. This comparison is useful because it provides for reflection on the international laws written explicitly to protect civilians during war because of the devastation to the European continent during World War II.

When American soldiers intentionally kill civilians of the population that needs protection, or otherwise violate the tenets of the Geneva Conventions, the media invites domestic and international responses, publicizing the debate. In the United States during World War II, the American public saw mostly to its own interpretation of civilian casualty events and the war in general. Now, because of the Internet, the American public accesses a plethora of international perspectives and opinions of its worldwide military commitments, and these reports are not always favorable. Nonetheless, the global media tells a story that influences both American public opinion and that of the local populations where the civilian casualty events took place. The resulting discourse highlights a perceived disconnect between American political messaging and some activities of military units in the theater of operations. Political leaders of America have always declared their commitment to protecting human rights in the many nations where the U.S. military deploys its troops, yet incidences of Americans killing members of the protected population continue to occur. Some recent examples are the Haditha killing of twenty-four Iraqi civilians in 2005[15], the gang rape/murder case involving a fourteen-year-old Iraqi girl and her family in 2006[16], the Kandahar 'thrill' killings of 2010[17], and the

---

[15] For further reading on the 2005 Haditha massacre, consult Ellen Knickmeyer, "In Haditha, Memories of a Massacre," *The Washington Post* online (May 27, 2006), accessed December 20, 2011 http://www.washingtonpost.com/wp-dyn/content/article/2006/05/26/AR2006052602069.html; Scott Pelley, "Haditha Massacre Defendant: We Did What We Had To," *CBS News* online (January 6, 2012), accessed January 10, 2012 http://www.cbsnews.com/8301-18563_162-57354199/haditha-massacre-defendant-we-did-what-we-had-to/.
[16] Ellen Knickmeyer, "Details Emerge in Alleged Army Rape, Killings," *The Washington Post* online (July 3, 2006) accessed February 20, 2012, http://www.washingtonpost.com/wpdyn/content/article/2006/07/02/AR2006070200673_pf.html; Joshua Hammer, "Death Squad," book review of *Black Hearts: One Platoon's Descent Into Madness in Iraq's*

alleged killing of sixteen Afghan civilians in early March 2012.[18] Why is it important for American soldiers to refrain from harming civilians during combat operations?

American soldiers should refrain from harming civilians during combat operations because it is counterproductive to mission accomplishment and results in a decline in support for military intervention forces. This can have lasting effects on foreign policy. Reducing civilian casualties is a moral and strategic issue, and should be analyzed separately from the other aspects of military operations. Political and military leaders must make civilian casualty avoidance an important goal during war. The U.S. Army must avoid the intentional killing of civilians because of the media's ubiquitous influence, international political implications, and its adverse effects on the increasing complexity of military operations.

> Today's history is written the very moment it happens. It can be photographed, filmed, [and] recorded…It can be transmitted immediately through the press, radio, [and] television. It can be interpreted, heatedly discussed.[19]
>
> Valerie Alia, *Media Ethics and Social Change*

Media Influence

Triangle of Death by Jim Frederick posted on *The New York Times* online, Sunday Book Review (March 11, 2010), accessed February 22, 2012, http://www.nytimes.com/2010/03/14/books/review/Hammer-t.html.

[17] "Soldier Gets Life Sentence in Afghan Thrill-Killings," *Fox News* online (November 10, 2011), accessed January 15, 2012 http://www.foxnews.com/us/2011/11/10/soldier-found-guilty-in-afghan-thrill-killings/; Luke Mogelson, "A Beast in the Heart of Every Fighting Man," *The New York Times* online, (April 27, 2011), accessed December 20, 2011 http://www.nytimes.com/2011/05/01/magazine/mag-01KillTeam-t.html?pagewanted=1&_r=2&ref=calvingibbs.

[18] Taimoor Shah and Graham Bowley, "U.S. Sergeant is Said to Kill 16 Civilians in Afghanistan," *The New York Times* online (March 11, 2012), accessed on March 15, 2012 at http://www.nytimes.com/2012/03/12/world/asia/afghanistan-civilians-killed-american-soldier-held.html?pagewanted=1&_r=1.

[19] Valerie Alia, *Media Ethics and Social Change*, (New York: Routledge, 2004), 1.

On January 3, 2004 around 11 PM, Iraqi cousins, Marwan and Zaydoon Fadhil, returned to their hometown of Samarra from their day of work in Baghdad when U.S. soldiers on patrol pulled the cousins over at a checkpoint. Because the soldiers did not speak Arabic and the Iraqi cousins did not speak English, it was hard for the soldiers to determine why the cousins were out after curfew. However, after attempts at questioning the Iraqis and searching their vehicle, the soldiers released them. Immediately after the cousins got back into their truck, the soldiers' platoon leader radioed from his visible but distant position, directing that the soldiers detain the cousins at once. The soldiers then apprehended the cousins and took them to the bank of the Tigris River. At gunpoint, the soldiers told Marwan and Zaydoon to jump into the water. Marwan survived and Zaydoon's body washed ashore about twelve days later. The incident was escalated to top military leaders in Iraq and then to the American media.[20] What are the media implications of U.S. soldiers harming civilians?

The drowning incident, (although it involved only one civilian casualty) was clearly not done in self-defense, and therefore proved to be counterproductive to the military intervention mission in Iraq because it caused the local population to call into question the American values of "democracy and human rights."[21] As the case against the soldiers progressed, subsequent articles informed the public that the soldiers involved were charged with committing crimes and therefore held accountable for their actions. Additionally, the release of this story came in the wake of the discovery of the abuses committed at Abu Ghraib, which forced the American public to question the values of its service members serving in harm's way.[22]

The media influences public opinion about civilian casualty events and the nature of ongoing conflicts by offering multiple perspectives, which is the principle difference between now and the

---

[20] Dexter Filkins, "The Fall of the Warrior King," *The New York Times Magazine*, (October 23, 2005), accessed January 7, 2012 http://www.nytimes.com/2005/10/23/magazine/23sassaman.html?pagewanted=all.

[21] "'Drowned Iraqi' Was Forced into River by Five U.S. Soldiers," (February 14, 2004), *The Independent* online, accessed March 19, 2012 at http://www.islamweb.net/ehajj/printarticle.php?id=57166&lang=E.

[22] "U.S. Soldier: Drowning was Ordered," (July 28, 2004), posted on *Aljazeera* online, accessed March 19, 2012 at http://www.aljazeera.com/archive/2004/07/2008410102250891881.html.

World War II era. Back then, the mainstream media garnered public support for the war effort mentioning neither the brutality of combat nor the impact of the war on foreign civilians. Over time, the media gained autonomy and grew tremendously from newspapers and radio to television and the Internet, which, beginning with online coverage of the Global War on Terror in 2003, eventually led to its current state of information overload. The ubiquitous nature of the contemporary media provides consumers unlimited access to civilian casualty-related information instantly, giving military and political leaders very little time to investigate and respond to the public once stories are released. An example, discussed later, is a piece on drone strikes in Pakistan and their effects on the local civilians. A mitigating factor, which may be a counterbalance to the media's interpretation of civilian casualty events is the emergence of social media. The military uses social media to encourage discourse between the local population and members of the armed forces serving among them in the hopes of promoting stability and preventing civilian casualties.

The *New York Times Magazine* published an article about the vignette presented above, however, the article also introduces the reader to the commander of the unit, who by all accounts was very successful and served his country honorably. In the article, the American public learned of his accomplishments within his sector of Iraq preceding the drowning incident and how he and his unit performed two simultaneous and difficult missions, which involved securing the population and going after an enemy that blended in with (and lived among) the local population. Because the enemy did not wear uniforms, military units on the ground developed methods for identifying "good guys" and established intelligence gathering networks among the population to aid in the accomplishment of both missions. The Bush administration's policy on denying "unlawful combatants" privileges as prisoners of war under the Geneva Conventions[23] enabled troops freedom of maneuver to accomplish

---

[23] Craig R. Whitney, *The Abu-Ghraib Investigations: The Official Reports of the Independent Panel and the Pentagon on the Shocking Prisoner Abuse in Iraq,* Ed. Steven Strasser (New York: Public Affairs, 2004), Appendix B, 176.

these missions, however, the policy contributed to the ambiguity on the ground with regard to the treatment of civilians. The article is summarized below.

In his book, *Warrior King: The Triumph and Betrayal of an American Commander in Iraq*, Lieutenant Colonel Nathan Sassman, commander of the soldiers involved, shared his version of the story. Earlier that same January day (see vignette above), Sassman and his unit attended the memorial ceremony for one of his subordinates, Captain Eric Paliwoda, whose heart had been punctured by shrapnel during a recent attack. The attack that killed Paliwoda occurred in the wake of a realization that the war in Iraq was not the predicted short war against a uniformed army where the U.S. led multinational coalition would execute a regime change followed by a peacekeeping mission. The emergence of a violent Iraqi insurgency surprised American commanders and the Bush administration. Service members in Iraq were then urged to "increase lethality and go after the enemy" by the Fourth Infantry Division Commander, Major General Raymond Odierno.[24] According to Sassman, his sector of Iraq was like "Jekyll and Hyde" because by day they were "putting on a happy face" (conducting nation building activities related to stimulating the economy and restoring governance), and "by night," they "were hunting down and killing [their] enemies" (conducting counterinsurgency activities, which involved entering homes and detaining suspected members of the insurgency).[25] The difficulty lies in the fact that Sassman and his men had "virtually no training in building a new nation or conducting guerilla war."[26] Nonetheless, changes in the operational environment did not provide sufficient justification to military and political leaders for the killing of a civilian, albeit unintentional.

Intended or not, the noncommissioned officer who gave the order to push the Iraqis into the river, Sergeant First Class Tracy Perkins, was convicted in a general court martial hearing of aggravated assault, aggravated assault consummated by battery, and obstruction of justice. As a

---

[24] Dexter Filkins, "The Fall of the Warrior King," *The New York Times Magazine* (October 23, 2005), accessed January 7, 2012 http://www.nytimes.com/2005/10/23/magazine/23sassaman.html?pagewanted=all.
[25] Ibid.
[26] Ibid.

result, he was sentenced to six months in prison, reduced one pay grade to staff sergeant, and ordered to forfeit one month's pay.[27] Sassman was granted immunity as a result of his testimony at a 2004 Article 32 hearing (similar to a civilian grand jury session).[28] The overall message in the American media at the time was that war in Iraq was changing, which presented a tough challenge even for the military's best leaders, but that violence against civilians was reprehensible.

The Arab media's perspective is important to the current study of civilian casualty avoidance for two reasons. First, because the media influences the civilian population, and second, because the media is, at times, exploited by members of terrorist organizations who use local civilians as surrogate victims for their cause.[29] The local media is a good source to get an understanding of what the locals say about how the military intervention force treats civilians. The Arab world is still grappling with the relationship between terrorism and the military intervention force because, theoretically, citizens *should* have the right to resist foreign occupation with force, however, the forces that rise up in resistance to foreign occupation tend to be the same ones that instigate terrorism.[30]

Regarding the Fadhil vignette above, an Arab media source reported two negative comments about the American forces involved in the incident. First, the surviving cousin, Marwan, claimed that the American soldiers were laughing as they pushed the Iraqis into the river. Second, a possible justification for the event altogether was that the "worn-down, angry" U.S. soldiers stationed in Samarra faced daily grenade and roadside bomb attacks, which may have explained why they

---

[27] L.M. Otero, "Army Sergeant Sentenced to Six Months," *USA Today* (January 8, 2005), accessed January 7, 2012 http://www.usatoday.com/news/world/iraq/2005-01-08-soldier-drowning_x.htm; "6 Months for GI in Iraqi Drowning," *CBS News*, re-released (February 11, 2009), accessed January 7, 2012 http://www.cbsnews.com/stories/2005/01/05/iraq/main664951.shtml.

[28] "Cover-up of Iraq Bridge Incident Admitted," *USA Today* (July 30, 2004), accessed Janjuary 7, 2012 http://www.usatoday.com/news/nation/2004-07-30-drowning-confession_x.htm.

[29] Mohammed el-Nawawy, Ph.D., "Terrorist or Freedom Fighter?: The Arab Media Coverage of "Terrorism" or "So-Called Terrorism,"" *Global Media Journal*, Vol 3, Issue 5, (Fall 2004) accessed February 10, 2012 http://lass.calumet.purdue.edu/cca/gmj/fa04/gmj-fa04-elnawawy.htm.

[30] Ibid.

"wanted to teach a couple of Iraqis a lesson."[31] This characterization does not indicate an appreciation for intervention forces, and likely spread animosity for Americans among the local population.

Evidence suggests that the Arab media describes the West as a great enemy, and that the Western media stereotypes Arabs and Muslims as alien, violent strangers, intent upon battling non-believers throughout the world.[32] Ironically, studies show that overall Arab opinion about American freedom, democracy, people and education are favorable while the negative portrayal of America in Arab media stems from widely held beliefs about unfair policies pertaining to the treatment of Arabs,[33] as well as "inconsistent and biased United States Middle East foreign policy."[34] These points of view presented in the media influence the public as well as policy makers in both the United States and throughout the Arab world. Consequently, the ubiquitous global media is a double-edged sword, but understanding how foreign media portrays domestic issues and how it describes foreign relations is critical in gaining a holistic viewpoint on public support during war.

Dubbed "the Good War," fought by "the Greatest Generation,"[35] America entered World War II in order to preserve democracy and protect the United States; but if the public saw the human devastation caused by the war, would the war have been so collectively supported? World War II veteran, Edward W. Wood, Jr., wounded by artillery fire during the liberation of France from the Nazis in September 1944, argues that Americans believe (since World War II) that war leads to

---

[31] Ibid.

[32] Ashraf Galal, et al., "The Image of the United States Portrayed in Arab Online World Journalism," available online at http://online.journalism.utexas.edu/2008/papers/GalalPaper.pdf, accessed December 10, 2011, p2. This paper was submitted for consideration to the Ninth International Symposium on Online Journalism at the University of Texas at Austin, April 4-5, 2008.

[33] Ibid., 10.

[34] Ibid., 12.

[35] Edward W. Wood, Jr., *Worshipping the Myths of World War II: Reflections on America's Dedication to War* (Washington, D.C.: Potomac Books, Inc., 2006), 19. The author refers to nicknames commonly used to describe the World War II generation today, which originated from other authors. *The Good War* was an idea conceived by Stud Turkel, and later became a book in 1984. Wood also references Tom Brokaw's and Stephen Ambrose's characterization of "the Greatest Generation" as having been soldiers who returned to the United States after World War II seemingly untouched by what they'd seen and done in combat. Ambrose and Brokaw justified their high regard for WWII veterans by giving credit to them for stimulating the postwar domestic economy, medical breakthroughs, new art and literature, as well as providing the impetus for civil rights legislation (pp 79-80).

14

justice because of national beliefs in myths that mask the real nature of war.[36] The media, in all its forms, portrayed the Second World War to the American public without the brutality, and without the plight of civilians who lived where the enemy operated. Even war correspondents, such as Edward R. Murrow, who braved London air raids, reported the war to America in such a way that maintained public support and belief in the ideological reasons for fighting it.[37]

For example, historian, Michael Howard, who fought in the Italian campaign during World War II, suggested the examination of pre-war editorials in order to determine how war reporting justified the war effort and all its implications to readers.[38] The review of pre-World War II mainstream newspaper articles illustrates Howard's point. For example, in May 1944, during a speech given by Louis Nizer, he warned that the Germans planned to wage a third world war—while World War II was still being fought. He also said that "Germany [was] deliberately slaughtering and starving out the civilian population of Europe, not in order to win [the] war but to prepare her population predominance for the next [war]."[39] Albeit sensationalistic, Nizer's position probably incited panic, increased anti-German sentiment, and garnered American support for the war effort simultaneously. Not all of America supported its entrance into World War II, however, because some did not see the need to get involved, opposed conscription, protected conscientious objectors, and even sought an

---

[36] Edward W. Wood, Jr., *Worshipping the Myths of World War II: Reflections on America's Dedication to War* (Washington, D.C.: Potomac Books, Inc., 2006), ix-xi. The four myths are: (1) "The Good War," belied by the killing of innocents, by the nature of killing in WWII, and by what really happened to those hurt in combat; (2) "The Greatest Generation," is disproved by the reality behind the war movies, memoirs, and novels; the discussion shows how the generation that fought the war also helped defeat the hope for peace that swept the world at the end of WWII; (3) "We Won the War Largely on Our Own," we often tend to neglect the enormous contributions of Britain, the USSR, and China who fought a far longer war, suffered far higher casualties, and the obliteration of their urban and natural environment; (4) "When Evil Lies in Other, War is a Means to Justice," a belief inherited from WWII and its Holocaust is questioned, as is the notion that compromise and cooperation are always appeasement; only war is the solution to those regimes that make atrocities or threaten world peace, claims the myth (13-14).

[37] Robert E.Denton, Jr., Ed., *The Media and the Persian Gulf War* (Westport, CT: London: Praeger, 1993), 62.

[38] Michael Howard, "Reflections on the First World War" in Michael Howard (ed.), *Studies in War and Peace* (London 1970), 101-2.

[39] "Reich Already Plans New War, Author Tells Legion Leaders," *The Washington Post*, (May 1, 1944), 1.

antiwar amendment to the Constitution.[40] Subsequently, the antiwar effort almost completely

dissolved after the bombing of Pearl Harbor on December 7, 1941, and from that point on it seemed

the nation was mobilized (and encouraged by the media) to fight a total war. [41]

On D-Day (June 6, 1944), General Eisenhower broadcast via radio informing listeners that

the Allied landing in France was "part of the concerted United Nations plan for the Liberation of

Europe" and that "all patriots, men and women, young and old, have a part to play in the achievement

of final victory."[42] Reports published the numbers of Allied planes flown, and how many thousand

tons of bombs the Allies dropped on enemy targets, yet never with any mention of such statistics as

the approximately 60,000 French civilians killed by Allied bombs during the course of "liberating"

France in the first days of the Second World War.[43] Rather, the news remained focused on the Allied

campaign to liberate the victims of the Axis stronghold, however, many civilians who were not part

of the war effort—and therefore rarely, if ever, mentioned in the media—became casualties of war.

On August 7 and 8, 1945 front page headlines read, "Single Atomic Bomb Shakes Japan With Force

Mightier Than 20,000 Tons of TNT to Launch New Era of Power;"[44] "estimated total annihilation

area…was 200 yards in diameter;"[45] "Atom Bomb Erases 60 Pct. Of Jap City of 340,000; Much of

Rest is Damaged;" "More Than 4 Square Miles of Hiroshima Destroyed; Fliers Report Target Area

Dissolved in Smoke Cloud."[46]

These headlines, written strangely matter of fact, trivialized the large number of civilian

casualties "erased" all at once in Europe and Japan. However, one could argue that the American

government dropped the atomic bomb in retaliation to the bombing of Pearl Harbor under the

---

[40] Margaret A. Blanchard, *Revolutionary Sparks: Freedom of Expression in Modern America* (Oxford University Press: NC, 1992), 189.

[41] Ibid., 192.

[42] "Get Back From the Coast, Eisenhower Tells Europeans," *The Washington Post*, (June 6, 1944), 1.

[43] Stephen A. Bourque, Ph.D., "Operational Fires: Lisieux and Saint Lo – The Destruction of Two Norman Towns on D-Day," *Canadian Military History*, vol. 19, no. 2 (Spring 2010), 26.

[44] "Single Atomic Bomb Shakes Japan With Force Mightier Than 20,000 Tons of TNT to Launch New Era of Power," *The Washington Post*, (August 7, 1945), 1.

[45] Ibid

[46] *The Washington Post*, (August 8, 1945), 1.

impression that the entire Japanese population mobilized for war. These headlines were a form of propaganda, in Latin, called *suppressio veri* and *suggestio falsi*, which means to say things that are true while suppressing other truths in such a way that creates a false impression.[47] That false impression was that the Allies were fighting a world war to protect human rights and innocent civilians against the evils of the Axis powers. However, the reality was that the civilian populations living and dying in the area of operations (France, Germany, Japan, and Italy) were invisible in the American media.

Why did the American public support a strategy during World War II that killed hundreds of thousands of European civilians? One explanation is the interaction between the Office of War Information (OWI) and the Hollywood movie industry through which the nation's propaganda campaign delivered wartime entertainment films.[48] President Franklin D. Roosevelt instructed the Office of War Information to implement a program through the press, radio, and motion pictures to portray his justification for the war because he believed that movies were among the most effective means of reaching the American public.[49] By establishing the Bureau of Motion Pictures, the administration was able to communicate a narrative that explained how the United States was fighting an honorable war in response to an attack, and that it would win. In the script for the movie, *Bombardiers*, a pilot expressed concern about bombing innocent civilians, so the OWI suggested a script revision introducing the 'just war' concept (which justified the use of force at unprecedented levels) where enemy targets were *everywhere* and that the military tried to be, but was not always, surgically precise when bombing its military targets.[50] This adaptation gave the American public an example of what the administration viewed as its just war, yet never showed the destruction on the ground (in the media or in movies) after the bombs were dropped.

---

[47] Randal Martin, "A Brief History of Propaganda," published in *Censored 2012: Sourcebook for the Media Revolution* by Mickey Huff and Project Censored (Seven Stories Press; New York, 2011), 294).
[48] Clayton R. Koppes and Gregory D. Black, "What to Show the World: The Office of War Information and Hollywood, 1942-1945," *The Journal of American History*, Vol. 64, No. 1 (June 1977), 87.
[49] Ibid., 88-89.
[50] Ibid., 95.

Although the popular media did not transmit overt messages claiming that some populations versus others were expendable during World War II, the underlying message was that some had to pay the inevitable price of war with their lives. However, the media has evolved since World War II in several ways. From the "Five O'clock Follies" during the Vietnam War where the media broadcast atrocities and body counts from Saigon,[51] to the footage provided by Commanding General Norman H. Schwarzkopf during the first Gulf War in 1991 of precision-guided munitions streaking toward their targets,[52] the world finally saw the reality of war. The media, which evolved into a more independent actor particularly during international conflicts, still felt inhibited.

After the first Gulf War, executives from major news organizations (i.e. *Time, Newsweek, The Associated Press, The Washington Post, The New York Times, Los Angeles Times, The Wall Street Journal,* and *Chicago Tribune*) petitioned the Department of Defense to allow less restricted access to its operations. This resulted in an agreement called *Principles for News Media Coverage of DoD Operations.*[53] Continued evolution occurred to the media enterprise when the United States became involved in subsequent conflicts such as Somalia in 1992, Haiti in 1994, and Bosnia in 1995. It was during Operation Allied Force in Kosovo in 1999 when tight U.S. press restrictions caused the media to obtain information on a collateral damage incident—covered and sensationalized by enemy media—to be broadcast to the American public. Of this incident, Allied Force Commander, Admiral James Ellis, said:

---

[51] Christopher Paul, *Reporters on the Battlefield: The Embedded Press System in Historical Context* (California: RAND, 2004), 38.

[52] Ibid., 44; Robert E. Denton, Jr., Ed., *The Media and The Persian Gulf War* (Connecticut: Praeger Publishers, 2003).

[53] Ibid., 46. The guiding principles of this document were (1) independent reporting will be the primary means of coverage; (2) the use of pools is not to be encouraged, but they may be necessary for early access; when used, they should be disbanded as early as possible; (3) logistical constraints may mandate the use of pools; (4) a system of credentials will be established, with expulsion for violators; the media will attempt to assign experienced reporters to combat operations; (5) reporters will have access to all major military units, excluding special operations; (6) escorts should not interfere with reporting; (7) the military is responsible for pool transportation and should attempt to give reporters rides whenever possible; (8) the military should facilitate rapid media communications; and (9) the principles will also apply to the standing DoD National Media Pool systems (The Pentagon Pool).

The enemy was much better at this than we were…and far more nimble. The enemy deliberately and criminally killed innocents by the thousands, but no one saw it…We accidentally killed innocents, sometimes by the dozens, and the world watched it on the evening news.[54]

These incidences left the American public somewhat confused about operations in Kosovo, yet still supportive of intervention efforts. As the press continued to gain autonomy from government control and military influence over the next few years, and as the Internet began providing information and connecting people worldwide, the American public began to pursue its own alternatives to traditional media outlets. When the polarizing global media debate began confusing the public in the year leading up to the 2003 Iraq War,[55] Americans turned to the Internet for multiple sources of information that traditional radio, television, and print media did not provide.

According to polling done by the Pew Internet & American Life Project, during the terrorist attacks on September 11, 2001 and at the start of the Iraq War in March 2003, Americans used the Internet as a source for information about the war.[56] Overall, the Project's research showed that those who got their news over the Internet increased 70% from fifty-four million in March of 2000 to ninety-two million June of 2004. Polls conducted when fighting and violence increased during Operation Iraqi Freedom in 2003 suggested Americans used the Internet for another reason, as a unique source for photographic information not covered by the mainstream media.[57] Essentially, the Internet empowers the public to choose its own source of media, and to find information withheld or not available in traditional sources.

---

[54] Ibid., 49-50.

[55] Ernest A. Hakanen and Alexander Nikolaev, *Leading to the 2003 Iraq War: The Global Media Debate*, Palgrave Macmillan, Gordonsville, VA (2006), 3. Issues related to international political resistance to preemptive war, the relevance of the United Nations, the presence in Iraq of weapons of mass destruction, and Iraq's supposed linkages to Al Qaeda were frequently debated the year before the U.S. invasion of Iraq.

[56] Deborah Fallows and Lee Rainie, "The Internet as a Unique News Source," Pew Internet and American Life Project, July 8, 2004, accessed December 20, 2011, http://www.pewinternet.org/Reports/2004/Internet-as-Unique-News-Source/3-The-new-experience-of-war-images-online/1-Americans-are-turning-to-the-Internet-for-news-coverage-not-in-the-mainstream-news-media.aspx.

[57] Ibid.

Because of global connectivity to the Internet, the public pressures the American government to evaluate and comment on the behavior of those portrayed in videos and pictures filmed from the tactical edge of the battlefield. An example of this was the case regarding a video posted on the Internet in early January 2012 where four U.S. Marines were filmed urinating on dead bodies, presumably Taliban insurgents they'd just killed in Afghanistan.[58] Although an investigation is currently underway to determine the facts of the case, some or all of the Marines involved with the making of the video could be punished under the Geneva Conventions for the desecration of dead bodies, which is considered a war crime.

The immediate international response to the public release of photographic evidence of incidents like this illustrates the power of media. This type of behavior, reminiscent of Abu Ghraib, influences public opinion and encourages American leaders at the highest level to reassure the American people that such actions are not the norm.[59] Another example of the perceived American mistreatment of civilians portrayed in the media is collateral damage caused by drone strikes in Pakistan.

Local journalist from Waziristan, Noor Behram, wanted to share the local civilians' side of the story. He photographed the scene of sixty different drone strikes near northwest Pakistan immediately following the attacks. He found that far more civilians are being injured or dying than the American and Pakistani governments admit.[60] Behram claims that reporters do not always travel to the scene of the explosion, and therefore could not know whether the strikes actually killed insurgents or ordinary people living in Waziristan despite what they report. Behram estimates that

---

[58] Graham Bowley and Matthew Rosenbert, "Video Inflames a Delicate Moment for U.S. in Afghanistan," The New York Times online (January 12, 2012), accessed January 13, 2012 http://www.nytimes.com/2012/01/13/world/asia/video-said-to-show-marines-urinating-on-taliban-corpses.html?pagewanted=1&_r=1.

[59] Cindy Adams, "Hillary Clinton and Leon Panetta Condemn Marines Urinating on Taliban (video)," accessed January 13, 2012 http://www.examiner.com/us-headlines-in-national/hillary-clinton-and-leon-panetta-condemn-marines-urinating-on-taliban-video.

[60] Saeed Shah and Peter Beaumont, "US Drone Strikes in Pakistan Claiming Many Civilian Victims" (July 17, 2011), accessed December 20, 2011 http://www.guardian.co.uk/world/2011/jul/17/us-drone-strikes-pakistan-waziristan.

"[f]or every ten to fifteen people killed, they maybe get one militant." The danger, he says, is that the locals become enraged after the drone strikes occur because they destroy known insurgent compounds *and* nearby occupied civilian dwellings. A way to provide an outlet for the local civilians who live in the area where drone strikes occur is to communicate their concerns with the military intervention force through social networking sites.

Commanders in Afghanistan currently address the issue of civilian casualty avoidance in the hopes of preventing future violence against the indigenous population. In May 2010, the International Security Assistance Force Joint Command Commander and Afghan leaders met in Kabul to discuss the improvement of counterinsurgency operations and the prevention of civilian casualties.[61] Colonel Bradley Weisz, Deputy Chief of Current Operations said, "We need to change the mindset of our troops to the counterinsurgency (COIN) approach of 'protecting the people,' and the best way to do that is by sharing best practices and improving overall COIN awareness."[62] The International Security Assistance Force Joint Commander, Lieutenant General David Rodriguez, suggested that Mobile Training Teams[63] continue "to bring back many good lessons of restraint and good decision making from our young soldiers."[64] The details about this meeting, along with a picture of Major General Rouzi (Commander of the Afghan National Police), in attendance with U.S. military leaders, were posted on the Afghanistan International Security Assistance Force's blog.[65] This blog also posts commander's public correspondence, media releases, news, as well as morning and afternoon staff updates on progress and insurgent attacks in each region.

The International Security Assistance Force headquarters has embraced the use of social media, using such tools as Facebook, to reinforce transparency, and uses the blog to broadcast all of

---

[61] "Leaders Tackle Counterinsurgency and Civilian Casualties," (May 16, 2010) , accessed December 20, 2011 http://www.isaf.nato.int/article/news/leaders-tackle-counterinsurgency-and-civilian-casualties.html.

[62] Ibid.

[63] Mobile Training Teams (MTT) are U.S. and Coalition forces designated to train the Afghan Army's military and police forces.

[64] "Leaders Tackle Counterinsurgency and Civilian Casualties"

[65] A blog (combination of the words "web" and "log") is a website where individuals and organizations post information, and typically encourage interactive feedback, accessed January 13, 2012 (http://www.rebeccablood.net/essays/weblog_history.html).

their news—especially that which reflects positively on the efforts of the coalition and the Afghans working together to solve problems. General David H. Petraeus advised the use of social media to set up networking sites to enhance unity of effort with not only the local population, but with coalition nations, other government agencies, and non-governmental organizations serving in the region.[66] Many military organizations worldwide are leveraging social media to communicate their efforts as well. Social networking can enhance national security by providing a medium to display information, influence public opinion, conduct research and analysis, and develop and implement policies; but for the approximately one billion people on the Internet, the global capacity to read and respond to public information is both the best—and the most risky—aspect of this new form of communication.[67]

This section illustrated the media implications of why harming civilians is counterproductive to mission accomplishment. The media, as an institution, gained autonomy since World War II and began to acknowledge civilian casualties by reporting multiple perspectives of international conflicts to the public. When stories get released to the media about U.S. service members killing civilians while deployed, senior military officials and government leaders not only acknowledge the tragedy apologetically, but they make a commitment to the world that American values do not allow for such misconduct. The media, once almost entirely censored by the government, is now a tool to hold the government (and its most powerful tool, the military) accountable for its actions. This becomes important in the next chapter about the political implications of civilian casualty avoidance.

The humanization of foreign civilians living in the area of operations is something the media has done well to emphasize. The Internet, is the information outlet for much of humanity across the globe. The proliferation of social networking provides an interactive, mass media repository for billions (or more) users to ask questions, find answers, voice concerns, and gain awareness. The ability to exploit the benefits of this new technology could possibly improve relations with local

---

[66] Thomas D. Mayfield III, "A Commander's Strategy for Social Media," *Joint Force Quarterly*, Issue 60, 1st Quarter 2011, 82-83.
[67] James Jay Carafano, "Mastering the Art of Wiki: Understanding Social Networking and National Security," *Joint Force Quarterly*, Issue 60, 1st Quarter 2011, 73.

populations in deployed environments and lessen the likelihood of the deliberate killing of civilians by the military intervention force.

> Time and again, members of the foreign policy elite have misperceived the world and misconstrued American interests, thereby exacerbating rather than alleviating threats. Time and again, they have misunderstood war and the consequences likely to flow from the use of force. The frequency with which senior U.S. officials have disregarded long-term goals in favor of what appears expedient in the short term calls into question the extent to which "strategy" as such actually figures into the making of policy.[68]

---

[68] Andrew J. Bacevich, Ed., *The Long War: A New History of U.S. National Security Policy Since World War II* (New York: Columbia University Press, 2007), xiii.

Political Implications

Allah Dad was a forty-five-year-old farmer from the Kalagi hamlet in Kandahar Province. One afternoon in January 2010, according to his wife, Mora, two young soldiers entered the home, took the man outside, and soon after began shooting. Mora said one of the soldiers was restraining her to prevent her from going outside until they heard an explosion. She broke free and was able to get out of the house when she saw her husband on the ground on fire. She then went on to describe how the soldiers searched her home but did not find anything. Later that day, her father, Abdullah Jan, and two tribal elders listened to the Afghan intelligence agent explain that Dad was killed because he threatened the soldiers with a grenade that went off accidentally killing him. Abdullah Jan reported to the local authorities that Dad was a *mullah* (local religious leader) in his village mosque and had no ties with the Taliban, and therefore no reason to threaten harm to American soldiers. An elder from the Maiwand District, Haji Hayatullah, commented on this and the other two killings committed by the same group of American soldiers that day:

> The Americans have killed many people who did not support the Taliban, which is painful for us and actually creates hatred toward Americans; and that is why there is little or no help to the Americans from civilians here.[69]

The family of Allah Dad, and that of the two other victims killed that day, Gul Mudin and Marach Agha, reportedly received $11,300 as compensation for the deaths of their loved ones.[70] The quote from the local man above indicates that the rural Afghan population has stopped supporting coalition efforts, particularly when members of the coalition intentionally kill civilian members of their community. What are the political implications of U.S. soldiers harming civilians?

When the U.S. military is conducting counterinsurgency operations in a foreign nation, killing local civilians (who are not insurgents) is in direct opposition to political messaging about

---

[69] Taimoor Shah and Alissa J. Rubin, "Relatives Tell of Civilians Killed by U.S. Soldiers," *The New York Times* online (October 4, 2010), accessed December 20, 2011 http://www.nytimes.com/2010/10/05/world/asia/05afghan.html?ref=calvingibbs.

[70] Ibid.

protecting the population. The local Afghan man's comment in the vignette above is an example of the consequences of harming the local civilian population, which subsequently leads to the political challenge of re-establishing credibility. This section will address the discourse related to civilian casualty avoidance at the political level, the post-World War II efforts to protect civilian populations through international law, as well as overcoming political challenges regarding how the military conducts interventions.

Defense Secretary Robert Gates apologized for civilian deaths in Afghanistan caused by coalition forces at a press conference in March 2011.[71] At an Afghan National Security Council meeting the day prior, then commander of the International Security Assistance Forces in Afghanistan, General David H. Petraeus apologized to the Afghan people for the deaths of Afghan civilians to which Afghan President Hamid Karzai replied, "The people of Afghanistan are tired of these incidents and excuses, and condemnations cannot relieve their pain."[72] This interchange between senior government officials indicates that the issue of civilian casualties resides at the highest political level where apologies, as well as promises to protect civilians, are made publicly.

Eight months later, the media reported the outcome of the trial of the service members responsible for the deaths of the Afghan civilians described in the vignette above. At his court martial hearing in November 2011, Army Staff Sergeant Calvin Gibbs, was convicted of murder and conspiracy and was sentenced to life in prison. He was the most senior in the group of five who were charged with the murders of these three Afghan civilians in Kandahar.[73] The investigation into this case revealed previous widespread misconduct among the troops of this unit during deployments, including drug use, the mutilation of Afghan remains, and the gang-beating of the soldier who

---

[71] Al Pessin, "Gates Apologizes for Afghan Civilian Deaths," *Voice of America* online (March 7, 2011), accessed January 21, 2012 http://www.voanews.com/english/news/asia/US-Defense-Secretary-Arrives-in-Kabul-Amid-Strained-Relations-117510188.html.

[72] Alissa J. Rubin, "Afghan Leader Calls Apology in Boys' Deaths Insufficient," *The New York Times* online (March 6, 2011), accessed January 21, 2012 http://www.nytimes.com/2011/03/07/world/asia/07afghanistan.html.

[73] "Soldier Gets Life Sentence in Afghan Thrill-Killings," *Fox News* online (November 10, 2011), accessed January 15, 2012 http://www.foxnews.com/us/2011/11/10/soldier-found-guilty-in-afghan-thrill-killings/.

reported the drug use to the chain of command. When the soldiers were asked why they were so easily talked into killing civilians, one of the soldiers replied, "the unit wanted action and firefights," but instead "found itself performing a more humanitarian, counterinsurgency mission."[74] His complaint about the nature of warfare illuminates a potential widespread misunderstanding regarding the mission in Afghanistan, despite assurance by the U.S. government that the military is there (trained) to protect the population. Furthermore, the Afghans (according to their president's comment above) do not want to lose any more civilians, whether killed intentionally or accidentally.

After a decade of American troops on the ground in Afghanistan, the political discourse resembles the challenge of reconciling two competing norms in international law: sovereignty and human rights.[75] The argument occurs when external intervention comprised of international organizations, or coalitions of the willing, share authority with the host nation government.[76] The argument is exacerbated when the intervention force kills civilians of the host nation (accidentally or intentionally), especially in the face of repeated declarations that democracy protects and promotes human rights.[77]

The U.S. military in Afghanistan initially conducted combat missions against known terrorist organizations, but since its arrival in 2001, it underwent a transition to reconstruction and stabilization missions.[78] Although international combat troops are operating in Afghanistan under a United

---

[74] "Soldier Gets Life Sentence in Afghan Thrill-Killings"

[75] Cristina Gabriela Badescu, *"Humanitarian Intervention and the Responsibility to Protect: Security and Human Rights"* (London and New York: Routledge, 2011), 19.

[76] Ibid., 25.

[77] Michael E. O'Hanlon, *Expanding Global Military Capacity for Humanitarian Intervention* (Washington, D.C.: Brookings Institution Press, 2003), 2.

[78] Donald Rumsfeld, Memorandum to the President re: Strategic Thoughts (September 30, 2001), available online at Rumsfeld.com, accessed February 25, 2012 http://library.rumsfeld.com/doclib/sp/272/2001-09-30%20to%20President%20Bush%20re%20Strategic%20Thoughts.pdf; Condoleeza Rice, Memorandum to Senior Political and Military Leaders re: Declaratory Policy on Afghanistan (September 27, 2001), available online at Rumsfeld.com, accessed February 25, 2012, http://library.rumsfeld.com/doclib/sp/1502/2001-09-27%20from%20Condoleezza%20Rice%20re%20Declaratory%20Policy%20on%20Afghanistan-%20Memo%20Attachment.pdf; Paul Wolfowitz, Memorandum to Secretary Rumsfeld re: Use of Special Forces, (September 23, 2001), available online at Rumsfeld.com, accessed February 25, 2012, http://library.rumsfeld.com/doclib/sp/267/2001-09-

Nations resolution until 2014,[79] because it is a member of the United Nations, Afghanistan is empowered to exercise jurisdiction within its territorial borders.[80] This means that the leaders of the Afghan government could leverage the United Nations to remove security forces earlier—despite progress made during reconstruction efforts, requesting to keep a small contingent for training purposes. Barring any major setbacks, the timeline set forth by the United Nations for the withdrawal of international combat troops will likely remain unchanged.

The concept of using military intervention for humanitarian purposes was a controversial topic in international relations before the attacks of September 11, 2001, but debates about the relevance of the United Nations reignited since the 2003 invasion of Iraq.[81] It is important to revisit the history of these peace conferences to remind ourselves that the goal of establishing an international forum for settling disputes was to regulate and/or *prevent* war. International concerns about how to mitigate violence against civilians during war began in the eighteenth century in the form of peace conferences. A review of the Hague and Geneva conventions as well as the post-World War II establishment of the United Nations, will provide context for the discussion of current and future political implications of civilian casualty avoidance.

At the Hague Convention of 1899, Russian Tsar Nicholas II proposed a declaration to ban the launching of "any kind of projectile [aimed at people below] and explosive from balloons, or by other methods of similar nature," such as poisonous gas.[82] Although the terms of the peace conference lasted only 5 years, it was a popular belief that the airplane would lead to a state of world peace by eliminating national borders thereby preventing future wars. The 'preventive' use of the airplane foreshadows a discussion of air power theory, which the following chapter covers. The second Hague

---

23%20from%20Wolfowitz%20re%20Using%20Special%20Forces%20on%20Our%20Side%20of%20the%20Line.pdf.

[79] "The International Afghanistan Conference Bonn 2011," posted on the United Nations Permanent Mission of Afghanistan to the United Nations in New York website (December 5, 2011), accessed January 24, 2012 http://www.afghanistan-un.org/2011/12/the-international-afghanistan-conference-bonn-2011/.

[80] *"Humanitarian Intervention and the Responsibility to Protect,"* 21.

[81] Ibid., 3.

[82] Yuki Tanaka and Marilyn B Young, eds., *Bombing Civilians, A Twentieth Century History* (New York: The New Press, 2009), 9.

Convention of 1907 established more rules of war and addressed the rights and obligations of neutral nations. The League of Nations, which ratified the Treaty of Versailles and ended World War I, was established a decade later. Its principle mission was to maintain peace through collective security and be the platform to settle international disputes through negotiation. Of its initial forty-two founding members, twenty-three remained until is dissolution in 1946.[83]

The Geneva Conventions and its subsequent additions are international treaties that protect people not taking part in fighting a war (i.e. civilians, medical personnel, and aid workers), as well as those who can no longer fight.[84] The fourth Geneva Convention afforded protection to civilians in civil wars, internal armed conflicts that spill over into other states, or conflicts in which third states or a multinational force intervenes alongside the government (i.e., Operations Iraqi Freedom and Enduring Freedom). It further required humane treatment and appropriate medical care for all prisoners of war. It specifically prohibits the murder, mutilation, torture, cruel and humiliating treatment of enemy prisoners, such as those held at Abu Ghraib and similar facilities, until President George W. Bush reclassified them as unlawful combatants thereby restricting the rights of those detained in connection with the Global War on Terror. Of the eleven resolutions of the conference, the eighth emphasizes the human suffering aspect of World War II, for military and civilians alike, and the commitment to avoid a similar war at all costs:

> The Conference wishes to affirm before all nations: that, its work having been inspired solely by humanitarian aims, its earnest hope is that, in the future, Governments may never have to apply the Geneva Conventions for the Protection of War Victims; that its strongest desire is that the Powers, great and small, may always reach a friendly settlement of their differences through cooperation and understanding between nations, so that peace shall reign on earth for ever [sic].[85]

---

[83] "The Avalon Project: Documents in Law, History, and Diplomacy," posted on the Yale Law School Lillian Goldman Law Library website, accessed January 24, 2012 http://avalon.law.yale.edu/subject_menus/lawwar.asp.

[84] "The Geneva Conventions of 1949 and Their Additional Protocols," posted on the International Committee of the Red Cross (ICRC) website (October 29, 2010), accessed on January 24, 2012 http://www.icrc.org/eng/war-and-law/treaties-customary-law/geneva-conventions/overview-geneva-conventions.htm.

[85] *Geneva Conventions of August 12, 1949 For the Protection of War Victims*, Department of State Publication 3938, General Foreign Policy Series 34 (August 1950), 22.

Adopted in 1949 (and yet to be superceded), the Geneva Conventions took into account all of the atrocities and human rights violations of World War II, the first of which to adjudicate was the one of the most unspeakable civilian casualty events in history, the Jewish Holocaust.[86]

More than six million Jews died in the Holocaust, which was nearly one-third of the world's Jewish population situated primarily in Europe.[87] When the state of Israel was formed after World War II, almost 374,000 Holocaust survivors entered the new country while approximately 150,000 others settled in America.[88] The mass migration of refugees was but one of the significant humanitarian consequences of Adolf Hitler's genocide campaign. Another was the punishment of those who took part in the administration of the concentration camps across Europe. The culmination of events, which took place at the end of World War II, was the basis for the establishment of the United Nations and its associated commissions.

As World War II approached its final months, the U.S. government took the lead in developing Allied war crimes policy under the auspices of the United Nations War Crimes Commission (UNWCC), which investigated allegations of war crimes (most of which involved killing civilians) committed by Nazi Germany and its allies.[89] The UNWCC began its work prior to the official establishment of the United Nations (UN). It was comprised of seventeen Allied Nations and engaged in formulating and implementing procedures to ensure the detection, apprehension, trial and punishment of the accused. In addition, the Commission developed principles for the new practice of international law and planning for international tribunals.[90] The major war criminals were tried at the International Military Tribunal (IMT) at Nuremberg. An International Tribunal for the Far East (IMTFE) was also established at this time. The four Allied powers could prosecute crimes at the IMT related to crimes against peace, war crimes, crimes against humanity, and participation in the

---

[86] Ibid.

[87] Donald M. McKale, *Hitler's Shadow War: The Holocaust and World War II* (Copper Square Press: New York, 2002), 454.

[88] Ibid., 456.

[89]"Ibid., 416-417.

[90] http://archives.un.org/ARMS/sites/ARMS/uploads/files/unwcc_finding_aid.pdf.

planning or conspiracy to commit the aforementioned crimes.[91] U.S. Treasury Secretary, Henry

Morgenthau (a German American Jew[92]), recommended that the President direct that all leaders

involved in the Holocaust be summarily shot, however Secretary of War, Henry Stimson, labeled

atrocities and waging wars of aggression as war crimes, and that the Nazi regime would be treated as

a criminal conspiracy.[93] As the international tribunals got underway, the United Nations was

officially established on October 24, 1945 in San Francisco, California, where fifty-one member

states signed a charter pledging to:

> save succeeding generations from the scourge of war, which twice in [their] lifetime brought
> untold sorrow to mankind; and to reaffirm faith in fundamental human rights, in the dignity
> and worth of the human person, in the equal rights of men and women and of nations large
> and small; and to establish conditions under which justice and respect for the obligations
> arising from treaties and other sources of international law can be maintained; and to promote
> social progress and better standards of life in larger freedom.[94]

The number one purpose of the United Nations is:

> To maintain international peace and security, and to that end: to take effective collective
> measures for the prevention and removal of threats to the peace, and for the suppression of
> acts of aggression or other breaches of the peace, and to bring about by peaceful means, and
> in conformity with the principles of justice and international law, adjustment or settlement of
> international disputes or situations which might lead to a breach of peace.[95]

At the time of its creation, UN member nations could visualize 'the scourge of war' as it

related to World Wars I and II. It made sense to place value on the 'faith in fundamental human

rights,' 'the dignity and worth of the human person,' as well as 'conformity with the principles of

justice and international law,' given the magnitude of the atrocities committed across Europe. The

signatories agreed that these principles were worth fighting for. Avoiding civilian casualties,

therefore, was an integral part of the underlying logic behind the creation of the United Nations.

---

[91] "Hitler's Shadow War," 417

[92] Dewey Browder, "Henry Morgenthau, Jr.: American Statesman and German American Jew," in Malcolm Muir, Jr., Ed., *The Human Tradition in the World War II Era* (Wilmington, DE: Scholarly Resources Inc., 2001), 101.

[93] Dough Linder, "The Nuremburg Trials," accessed January 28, 2012 http://archives.un.org/ARMS/sites/ARMS/uploads/files/unwcc_finding_aid.pdf.

[94] "Charter of the United Nations," *Handbook on the Peaceful Settlement of Disputes Between States* (New York: United Nations,1992), 155.

[95] Ibid.

Derived from the Geneva Conventions and the United Nations, the Department of Defense created the Law of War.[96]

The Law of War consists of four principles. First, military necessity, which prohibits intentional targeting of protected persons (i.e. civilians and those who have surrendered) and places (i.e. hospitals and schools) because they do not constitute legitimate military objectives. Second, the principle of unnecessary suffering forbids the use of weapons and ammunition in such a way that exceeds military necessity with regard to mission accomplishment. Third, the principle of distinction requires parties to a conflict to distinguish between combatants and noncombatants, and between protected property and places. This is perhaps the most challenging aspect of the law of war during counterinsurgency operations because the enemy blends with the population. Fourth, the principle of proportionality prohibits attacks expected to cause incidental loss of civilian life, injury to civilians, damage to civilian objects, or a combination thereof.[97] The Law of War provides guidelines inside which the military plans and executes its operational missions.

American service members who violate the Laws of War are criminally charged, but their cases are not sent to an international military tribunal; rather, their cases are heard in a trial by court martial, which falls under the Uniform Code of Military Justice (UCMJ).[98] This can be problematic because the U.S. military effectively opted out of utilizing the international court system and established a litigation process where the military sits in judgment of itself.[99] An example of a question left to the court martial authority to answer during trials on civilian casualties is whether at the time of the incident, it was clear what type of killing was inevitable and lawful, versus killing that

---

[96] Joint Publication 1-04, *Legal Support to Military Operations* (Washington, D.C.: Government Printing Office, 2011), II-2; see also Morris Greenspan, *Soldier's Guide to the Laws of War* (Washington, D.C.: Public Affairs Press, 1969).

[97] Ibid.

[98] Stjepan Mestrovic, Rules of Engagement? A Social Anatomy of an American War Crime: Operation Iron Triangle, Iraq (New York: Algora Publising, 2008), 159.

[99] Joseph Goldstein and Burke Marshall and Jack Schwartz, *The My Lai Massacre and Its Cover Up: Beyond the Reach of Law? The Peers Commission Report with a Supplement and Introductory Essay on the Limits of the Law* (New York: The Free Press, 1976), 4.

was a war crime.[100] Military courts may not be the best place to try war criminals because of the potential risks of a conflict of interest (i.e. a court martial convening authority realizes he or she is hearing a case about someone with whom they'd previously served or otherwise wished to protect).

In the post-Cold War era during the 1990s, political fragmentation, social upheaval, and nationalism, coupled with the rapid expansion of the interdependent global economy and the revolutions in international communications, resulted in a climate of uncertainty not predicted immediately following World War II.[101] Admiral Miller, Commander in Chief of the U.S. Atlantic Command and NATO's Supreme Allied Commander, Atlantic, argued that this type of challenge presented opportunities to limit regional disorder and to create new global cooperative networks to promote peace, prosperity, and justice.[102] However, according to Miller, the United Nations failed to provide a real collective security system when open hostilities erupted during the Cold War, which empowered the North Atlantic Treaty Organization[103] (NATO).[104] The strength of NATO versus the UN is its experience in commanding, and operating within, a joint, combined, multi-national environment.[105] However, the employment of NATO (seen as a military structure) in support of the UN (seen as a peacekeeping structure) leads to cognitive dissonance, which is historically associated with civilian casualty events. The debate about the nature of war, and which diplomatic tools to employ, is settled at the political level, but is there a better way to organize?

Two recommended restructuring concepts for military forces assigned to the missions of mediation, stabilization, and crisis resolution are (1) the creation of specialized units for peace-keeping, peace-enforcing, and peace-building missions (implemented by the Russian military), or (2)

---

[100] Ibid.

[101] Paul D. Miller, *Leadership in a Transnational World: The Challenge of Keeping the Peace* (Washington D.C.: The Institute for Foreign Policy Analysis, 2003), 1.

[102] Ibid.

[103] "A Short History of NATO," posted online under NATO History, accessed February 20, 2012, http://www.nato.int/history/nato-history.html; NATO was created in April 1949 to deter Soviet expansion, to forbid the revival of nationalist militarism in Europe through strong North American presence on the continent, and to encourage European political integration.

[104] *Leadership in a Transnational World: The Challenge of Keeping the Peace,* 11.

[105] Ibid., 20.

the adaptation of existing forces to meet those requirements (implemented by the American military).[106] Despite the agreed upon force structure, the challenge to overcome is the present view that when the UN has strong backing from the United States, that the nature of the conflict becomes an opportunity to pursue American, or Western, interests.[107] Further, it has been said that once the UN intervenes militarily in an emergency, *its actions become part of the problem* (resulting in an increase in civilian casualties).[108]

When engaged in the complicated amalgamation of tasks referred to as 'nation building,' the UN "not only seek[s] to keep the peace, they now often assume the role of police force and temporary judiciary," and take the lead in restructuring military forces, civil services, and other state institutions.[109] All of this is typically done in an unstable environment where belligerents blend in with the civilian population, which contributes to the difficulties associated with distinguishing combatants from civilians. Unity of effort among international forces and political leaders, to include the host nation, is essential for success in post-war intervention operations and the avoidance of civilian casualties.

This section described how harming civilians is counterproductive to mission accomplishment because it thrusts U.S. political and military leaders into a debate about their commitment to human rights versus their justification for the use of force. The discourse related to civilian casualty avoidance currently exists at the political level, yet subordinate echelons are long overdue to participate. Operational planners must take on the formidable task of passing foreign policy discourse down from the strategic level to the tactical level.

Studying the history of the humanitarian devastation felt across most of the European continent in the aftermath of World Wars I and II is key to understanding the global commitment to

---

[106] Ibid., 37.

[107] John Harriss, Ed., *The Politics of Humanitarian Intervention* (London: Pinter Publishers, 1995), 12.

[108] Ibid., 14.

[109] Adekeye Adebjo and Chandra L. Sriram, Eds., *Managing Armed Conflicts in the 21st Century* (London: Frank Cass Publishers, 2001), xiv.

the prevention of future world wars and the protection of civilians from future atrocities. Ironically, however, it seems as if an escalation of force (and an acceptance that there *will* be collateral damage) is the preferred method of settling post-Cold War disputes. Subsequently, the focus is less about prevention of war and more about how to organize military forces. Senior military leaders serving at the national level should mandate that discussions related to topics of civilian casualty avoidance, civil military relations, and the Law of War occur regularly to ensure that these lessons are not lost.

Protecting civilian populations and respecting human rights during war were the basis for the establishment of international law (Geneva Conventions), and multinational alliances (UN and NATO) were the enforcement mechanism. After nearly seventy years of interventions, the UN and NATO exist to cooperate, albeit sometimes in disagreement, for the settlement of international disputes by enforcing international law. When organized to conduct operations as a multinational coalition, it is imperative that the nature of the conflict (i.e. the transition from 'search-and-destroy' to 'clear-and-hold'[110] during the Vietnam War) is communicated to the entire organization, from the multi-national commanding general at the headquarters to the platoon leader leading troops and interacting with civilians on the ground.

---

[110] Lewis Sorley, *A Better War: The Unexamined and Final Tragedy of America's Last Years in Vietnam*, Orlando, Harcourt Inc. (1999), 7. Regarding his assessment of the nature of warfare during Vietnam, General Matthew Ridgway said at a Carnegie Endowment for Peace event, "The emphasis should not be on the military destruction of Communist forces in the South but on the protection of the people of South Vietnam and the stabilization of the situation at a politically tolerable level." This argument occurs today with regard to the mission in Afghanistan.

> [Moral factors] constitute the spirit that permeates war as a whole, and at an early stage they establish a close affinity with the will that moves the whole mass of force, practically merging with it, since the will itself is a moral quantity. Unfortunately they will not yield to academic wisdom. They cannot be classified or counted. They have to be seen or felt.[111]
>
> Carl von Clausewitz, *On War*

Complexity of Military Operations

Fourteen-year-old Abeer Qasim Hamza became aware that she had attracted the unwelcome attention of American soldiers manning a checkpoint she passed through daily in her village located in the city of Mahmudiyah, near Baghdad. The girl's mother, Fakhriyah, asked a neighbor if Abeer could start sleeping in their home because she believed her daughter was in danger. The neighbor, Omar Janabi, agreed, but reassured Fakhriyah that U.S. soldiers would not harm her daughter. The next day, March 12, 2006, four members of the 1st Battalion, 502nd Infantry Regiment of the 101st

---

[111] Carl von Clausewitz, *On War* (Princeton, New Jersey: Princeton University Press, 1976), 184.

Airborne Division,[112] wearing disguises, entered the home and grabbed Abeer. Three of the four took turns raping her while her parents and six-year-old sister were shot to death. When the soldiers were done with Abeer, they placed a pillow over her face and shot her, then set her body on fire.[113] In the months following Mahmudiya killings, members from Al-Qaeda abducted two soldiers from this particular unit (Private First Class Thomas Tucker and Private First Class Kristian Menchaca) who were subsequently filmed being beheaded; the narrator in the background called the desecration, "revenge for our sister who was dishonored by a soldier of the same brigade."[114]

A few weeks prior to committing these atrocities, Private First Class Steven D. Green (whose idea it was to commit the rape/murders) spoke with an embedded reporter at his patrol base twenty miles south of Baghdad, and said, "I came over here because I wanted to kill people."[115] The conversation moved on to war stories about the persistent danger and horrific living conditions in which the soldiers survived for the first six months of their year-long deployment. Green told the story of how a well-liked member of their unit, Sergeant Kenith Casica, had died in December (approximately two months prior to the interview) after being shot in the throat while manning a checkpoint. Green recalled comforting him as he took his last breaths, until "there wasn't nothing in his eyes." He said that was his worst experience yet in Iraq. Presumably, the rape and quadrupal murders he would commit in the coming weeks would have made it to the top of his worst yet experiences list. He also indicated his frustration with his perception of his chain of command's notion that it was ok for infantrymen like himself to be attacked all the time, but that they made a big deal when an Iraqi accidentally got shot.

---

[112] Jim Frederick, *Black Hearts: One Platoon's Descent into Madness in Iraq's Triangle of Death* (New York: Crown Publishing Group, 2010), xiii.

[113] Ellen Knickmeyer, , "Details Emerge in Alleged Army Rape, Killings," *The Washington Post* online (July 3, 2006) accessed February 20, 2012, http://www.washingtonpost.com/wpdyn/content/article/2006/07/02/AR2006070200673_pf.html.

[114] Frederick, *Black* Hearts, 314-315; Tim King, "Beheading Desecration Video of Dead U.S. Soldiers Released on Internet by Al Qaeda," *Salem News* online (July 11, 2006), accessed February 22, 2012 http://www.salem-news.com/articles/july112006/tucker_menchaca_71106.php.

[115] Andrew Tilghman, "I Came Over Here Because I Wanted to Kill People," *The Washington Post* online (July 30, 2006), accessed February 20, 2012 http://www.washingtonpost.com/wp-dyn/content/article/2006/07/28/AR2006072801492.html.

Green believed that they were "pawns for the [expletive] politicians, for people that don't give a [expletive] about [them] and don't know anything about what it's like to be out [there]."[116] Green's complaints about his leadership being pawns for politicians illustrates the cognitive dissonance which the young soldiers mentioned in this work have not been able to reconcile. Green is currently serving five consecutive life sentences with no possibility of parole; the other two soldiers who confessed to the rape and murder of Abeer and her family are serving a ninety-year sentence with the possibility of parole in twenty years, and a one-hundred-year sentence with the possibility of parole in ten years respectively.[117] What are the implications of harming civilians given the complexity of contemporary military operations?

This vignette, like the others presented in previous sections, reveals the complexity of military operations in an equally complex operational environment. All soldiers preparing for deployment to combat train with their units prior to departure, but in each case, a dismissal of morals and discipline occurred, which resulted in tragedy. Although situations similar to the one described above occur in most wars of the past, the media now reports it to the world almost immediately. The challenge for soldiers is the balance of morality with killing. This section will examine bombing strategy and the moral debate surrounding the targeting of civilians—to include a lesser known population "targeted" in the United States—during World War II, how current military doctrine *should* prepare the military for complex operations, and present examples which illustrate how harming civilians complicates the challenges of conducting intervention operations in a complex environment.

Airpower theorist, Giulio Douhet, published his famous treatise called *The Command of the Air* in 1921, in which his theory postulated the decisiveness of strategic bombing. Subsequently translated into English, French, German, and Russian, it was said to have influenced the thinking of

---

[116] Ibid.
[117] "The Blackest Hearts: War Crimes in Iraq"

aviators in various countries prior to World War II.[118] According to Douhet, with command of the air, a given nation's air force is free to operate whenever and wherever it desires, while the enemy's air capability is rendered helpless. Perhaps most profound of Douhet's ideas, he believed that all future conflicts would be unrestrained, total wars, and that there would no longer be a distinction between combatants and noncombatants. He concluded that wars could only be won by bombing operational targets, such as railroad junctions and depots, industry and government centers, and also by destroying the morale of the enemy at its weakest points—the civilian population centers (cities and towns).[119] To have the most devastating results when bombing a civilian population, he recommended employing explosives, incendiaries, and poisonous gas munitions during strategic attacks.

Douhet's theory and works have caused intense debate. Supporters of Douhet, proclaim he was "the first great air theorist" and "perhaps the most important."[120] Critics of Douhet said he was "the dark side of airpower" and that he articulated a vision glorifying the "knockout blow" with fleets of bombers prowling the skies, burning cities, and causing mass death. Regardless of the debate, Giulio Douhet vertically expanded and ethically polarized the battlefield, forever changing the way wars are fought and the way enemies, especially noncombatants, are attacked.

Historically, the argument was that if aerial bombing technology developed further, it could shorten military operations abroad, which would end wars quicker, and that aerial bombing was humane and justifiable because it caused fewer casualties; this is still argued today by the Obama administration for the use of drones.[121] The moral explanation is that dropping bombs whether from planes or drones provides psychological distancing and fragmentation of responsibility.[122]

---

[118] John F. Shiner, Colonel U.S. Air Force, "Reflections on Douhet, The Classical Approach," *Air University Review* (January-February 1986). http://www.airpower.au.af.mil/airchronicles/aureview/1986/jan-feb/shiner.html, accessed December 3, 2011.

[119] Shriner, "Relections on Douhet."

[120] Dudney, "Douhet," 64.

[121] Tom Engelhardt, "Going for Broke: Six Ways the AF-PAK War is Expanding," in Nick Turse, Ed., *The Case for Withdrawal From Afghanistan* (London: New York: Verso, 2010), 119.

[122] Jonathan Glover, *Humanity: A Moral History of the Twentieth Century* (Great Britain: Yale University Press, 1999) 79-80. Glover defines psychological distancing as circumstances that allow one to think of other human beings as less than human. This process starts in basic training where law abiding citizens are

Furthermore, it was a popular belief that the airplane, shortly after its invention in the early twentieth century, would lead to a state of world peace by eliminating national borders thereby preventing future wars.[123] History proves that statement wrong. Although charting a course toward world peace by eliminating national borders is an option that world powers should consider, current endeavors, beginning in World War II and still in existence today, focus on striking a balance between the principles of humanity and military necessity.[124] Why did military planning shift its focus from bombing military targets to bombing civilians?

Much has been written of the strategic bombing campaigns and their effects on civilians and the military during World War II. In September 1945, the War department published *The United States Strategic Bombing Survey,* which gave details on strategy and air power.[125] According to the survey, Allied airmen lost in action totaled 79,265 Americans and 79,281 British. Despite Allied casualties, Germany and Japan suffered tremendously. Nearly four million German 'dwelling units' (homes) were destroyed and some 300,000 civilians killed.[126] After nine months of air attack (including two atomic bombs), 330,000 Japanese civilians were killed, but not all died right away; the principal cause of civilian deaths during and after the atomic bomb attack was burns.[127] Overall, the bombing campaigns of World War II caused the deaths of more than one million civilians.[128] Referred to as an element of military coercion, air power strategy is successful "whether nuclear or conventional," because it "rests on the threat to inflict harm on civilians;" however emphasis is placed

---

trained to think in terms of "kill or be killed." Psychological distance from an aircraft makes one unable to see the faces of the women and children being burned by the bombs dropped.

[123] Ibid., 8.

[124] C.A.J. Coady, "Bombing and the Morality of War," in *Bombing Civilians: A Twentieth-Century History* (New York: London: The New York Press, 2009), 218.

[125] *The United States Strategic Bombing Survey* (September 30, 1945) 5-6. The roles of Allied air power were to partner with the Navy over the sea lanes; partner with the Army in ground battle; provide support during the invasions; provide reconnaissance; move troops and critical supplies; and attack the enemy's vital strength behind the battle line.

[126] Ibid., 5-6.

[127] Ibid., 92. A chapter titled "The Effects of the Atomic Bomb," on pages 96-107 give gruesome details of the destruction of the structures, land, and the human beings in the aftermath of the bombings.

[128] Hermann Knell, *To Destroy A City: Strategic Bombing and Its Human Consequences in World War II* (Cambridge: Da Capo Press. 2003), 1.

on "the exploitation of the opponent's *military* vulnerabilities (emphasis original)."[129] Later, the author says that "coercion seeks to achieve the same goals as war fighting, but at less cost to both sides."[130] Citizens of small towns such as Wurzburg, Germany, circa March of 1945, would tend to disagree.

Hermann Knell, a teenager at the time of the Wurzburg attack (a city of 107,000 inhabitants which was 89% destroyed), survived the bombings and remembered the end of World War II, which silenced the fighting, air-raid sirens, and the droning of bomber formations. Once their home was bombed out, or *dehoused*, as the British Royal Air Forced called it, he and his family began surviving in their garden house. He recalled how the entire nation was paying for what the government had done to neighboring nations, the world, and its very own citizens.[131] He questioned why so many civilian towns were bombed during the war, particularly his hometown, which was destroyed beyond military necessity, and why so little is known about it. In 1946, he recalled being deliberately run over by an American Army truck, which did not stop, leaving him lying in the rubble filled street with a broken leg.[132] Memories of his experience of American occupation coupled with his belief that the American and British leadership that planned and directed the bombing campaigns in Europe should be held accountable, inspired him to write his version of history.[133]

Another civilian population was "targeted" during World War II, who lived in the United States, but became disenfranchised after the bombing of Pearl Harbor in December of 1941: Japanese Americans. On February 17, 1942, President Franklin D. Roosevelt signed Executive Order 9066, which appointed Lieutenant General John L. DeWitt commander of the relocation camps that would

---

[129] Robert A. Pape, *Bombing to Win: Air Power and Coercion in War* (Ithaca and London, Cornell University Press: 1996), 1.
[130] Ibid., 13.
[131] *To Destroy A City: Strategic Bombing and Its Human Consequences in World War II*, 5.
[132] Ibid., 7.
[133] Ibid., 10.

house Japanese Americans evacuated from their homes on the West Coast.[134] Of the forced removal

and detention of more than 110,000 Japanese Americans, General DeWitt said before a congressional

committee, "A Jap's a Jap. They are a dangerous element…There is no way to determine their

loyalty…."[135] Several months before the bombing of Pearl Harbor, the president directed an inquiry

into the "Japanese situation" led by Republican businessman, Curtis B. Munson, who found after

meeting with many Japanese Americans that they were overwhelmingly loyal to the United States.[136]

After the Pearl Harbor attacks, all detainees were screened for 'disloyalty' and placed under the

jurisdiction of the Wartime Civilian Control Administration, which was staffed by the Army's

Western Defense Command. In the summer of 1942, control of the evacuated people shifted to a

civilian agency called the War Relocation Authority.[137] One way to prove their loyalty to America

(even those who were already U.S. citizens) was through service in the military, so the 100th

Battalion, made up of Japanese Americans from Hawaii, and the 442nd Regimental Combat Team,

made up of Japanese Americans from the West Coast internment camps were activated and began

rotations into the theater of operations.[138] The Japanese detainees were "resettled" (freed) at the end

of World War II. The White House apologized to all of the detainees forty-five years later:

> A monetary sum and words alone cannot restore lost years or erase painful memories; neither
> can they fully convey our Nation's resolve to uphold the rights of individuals. We can never
> fully right the wrongs of the past. But we can take a clear stand for justice and recognize that
> serious injustices were done to Japanese Americans during World War II. In enacting a law
> calling for restitution and offering a sincere apology, your fellow Americans have, in a very
> real sense, renewed their traditional commitment to the ideals of freedom, equality, and
> justice. You and your family have our best wishes for the future.
> Sincerely,
> GEORGE BUSH
> PRESIDENT OF THE UNITED STATES
> OCTOBER 1990[139]

---

[134] Thomas Hara, "The Hara Family: The Story of a Nisei Couple," in Malcolm Muir, Jr., Ed., *The Human Tradition in the World War II Era* (Wilmington, DE: Scholarly Resources Inc., 2001), 45.

[135] Ibid., 46.

[136] Eric L. Muller, *American Inquisition: The Hunt for Japanese American Disloyalty in World War II* (Chapel Hill, NC: The University of North Carolina Press, 2007), 15.

[137] Ibid., 21.

[138] Wendy NG, *Japanese American Internment During World War II: A History and Reference Guide* (Connecticut: London, Greenwood Press: 2002), 63.

[139] Ibid., 163.

Is there a difference between the civilian detainees held at Abu Ghraib and the innocent Japanese Americans held at the 'relocation centers?' Have the nation's leaders (military and civilian alike) once again used incarceration in such a way that will necessitate an apology? Linkages between the perceived disloyalties of American citizens immediately following the bombing of Pearl Harbor in 1941 connect to those four in ten Americans who admitted to feeling some prejudice toward Muslims in 2006.[140] In the aftermath of the September 11th attacks, many supported the idea of requiring all Muslims—U.S. citizens and aliens alike—to carry identification cards which would "prevent future terrorist attacks."[141] How do these beliefs manifest themselves in the minds of service members on the battlefields of Iraq and Afghanistan? Can a new strategy change the behavior of deployed soldiers who may intend to commit violent acts against the civilian population, despite their preexisting beliefs about the people they are fighting?

Field Manual 3-24, *Counterinsurgency*, created under the advisement of General David H. Petraeus, was published in December 2006. The purpose of this manual was to establish a foundation for study before deployment, and served as the basis for operations in theater. Additionally, the (counterinsurgency) 'COIN manual,' as it is called, institutionalized Army and Marine Corps knowledge of broad, historical trends that outline the factors motivating insurgents. One of the first points presented in the manual is that Western militaries often neglect the study of insurgency, but those forces who are able to overcome their institutional inclination to wage conventional war against insurgents have a better chance for success.[142] The publication of this manual was an effort to encourage forces in theater to adapt their tactics in order to achieve success.

The manual covers such theoretical underpinnings as how to establish unity of effort among civilian and military activities (chapter two), designing counterinsurgency campaigns and operations (chapter four), and maintaining leadership and ethics in counterinsurgency (chapter seven). It is

---

[140] *American Inquisition: The Hunt for Japanese American Disloyalty in World War II*, pp 146-147.
[141] Ibid.
[142] Field Manual 3-24, *Counterinsurgency*, (Washington, D.C.: Government Printing Office, 2006), ix.

accompanied by a second manual, FM 3-24.2, *Tactics in Counterinsurgency*, which offers tactical planning guidance (chapter four), offensive, defensive, stability operations, and support to host nation security forces guidelines (chapters five through eight). These manuals are the new "smart books" for military practitioners of the day, but paradoxically, the Bush administration entered office five years prior to the publication of the COIN manual on a platform that sought to minimize the use of U.S. troops in "nation building."[143] And so began the twenty-first century's first iteration of Army Transformation, (toward modular structures that could achieve swift victories—mass was replaced with mobility) which evolved into a modular force not necessarily designed to conduct stability operations characterized by sizeable ground forces on protracted deployments.[144]

After the attacks of September 11, 2001 until the time period immediately following the invasion of Iraq in 2003, the military found itself doing just what the administration *didn't* plan for, and with a smaller force. The solution was that many units in Iraq and Afghanistan (in response to increasing insurgent activity) began adopting a predominantly enemy-centric, "search-and-destroy," approach to their areas of operations. However, rooting out terrorists at the start of both conflicts, without fully understanding the adversary (second and third order effects), served to alienate civilians and generate more resistance forces.[145]

The solution to a lack of strategic guidance was the publication of an interim manual in October 2004, Field Manual 3-07.22, *Counterinsurgency Operations*, which led to the publication of the current COIN manual in December 2006. In December 2008, the Army published Field Manual 7-0, *Training for Full Spectrum Operations*, which opens by informing the reader that "the future will be an era of persistent conflict," and that "conflict will extend to areas historically immune from

[143] David H. Ucko, *The New Counterinsurgency Era: Transforming the U.S. Military for Modern Wars* (Washington, D.C.: Georgetown University Press, 2009), 47.
[144] Ibid., 56.
[145] Ibid., 61.

battle, including the homeland—the United States and its territories."[146] Although the latter

publication is actually a training manual, its opening statements about the nature of conflict may have

misled some to believe that full spectrum operations (FSO) was a strategy that replaced COIN, and

that an increase in lethality against the enemy was permissible because doctrine explicitly defined the

current era as one of persistent conflict. This confusion may have led to the dichotomy of practice

among deployed units in Iraq and Afghanistan (from 2004 to 2012) where commanders chose

whether they implemented "population-centric COIN" or "enemy-focused FSO." This string of

events created a strain on the force, which is undoubtedly a contributing factor—but not a

justification for—the criminal actions committed against civilians by American service members in

Iraq and Afghanistan.

 "The dynamic and ambiguous environment of modern counterinsurgency places a premium

on leadership at every level, from sergeant to general. Combat in counterinsurgency is frequently a

small-unit leader's fight; however, commanders' actions at brigade and division levels can be more

significant."[147] When engaged in combat, soldiers rely on their basic training, which condensed into a

simple phrase, says, "don't think, just do what you're told."[148] Inherent in that logic is a subordinate's

trust in his or her leaders. Therefore, the notion that in the heat of a counterinsurgency fight, soldiers

have an obligation to disobey unlawful orders (used as a defense strategy by commanders since the

Vietnam War era) is in direct opposition to 'don't think, just do what you're told.' Lieutenant

Calley's trust in his leader's guidance and demonstrated obedience during the My Lai massacre came

out during his cross-examination when he said, "I didn't discriminate between individuals in the

village. They were all the enemy, they were all to be destroyed."[149] Upon further analysis, Calley's

---

[146] Field Manual 7-0, *Training for Full Spectrum Operations* (Washington, D.C.: Government Printing Office, 2008), 1-1.

[147] *Counterinsurgency*, 7-1.

[148] Joseph Goldstein, Burke Marshall and Jack Schwartz, *The My Lai Massacre and Its Cover Up: Beyond the Reach of Law? The Peers Commission Report with a Supplement and Introductory Essay on the Limits of the Law* (New York: The Free Press, 1976), 8.

[149] Ibid., 9.

unquestionable compliance and lack of empathy likely stemmed from the fact that all Vietnamese were regarded as "gooks,"[150] who were given an opportunity to evacuate their villages, before they became "free-fire zones," in which anyone remaining (men, women, and children) *must* be enemy and would indeed be killed.[151] History confirms that commanders' actions, and guidance are, in fact, very significant.

In May of 2006, in preparation for Operation Iron Triangle in Samarra, Iraq, Colonel Michael D. Steele, commander of 3rd Brigade, 101st Airborne Division, gave a verbal order to kill every military-age Iraqi male on Objective Murray (because all personnel on the objective were confirmed as enemy combatants).[152] The soldiers who executed the mission encountered no resistance or hostility, and killed three of the prisoners they'd detained in order to remain in compliance with the brigade commander's (unlawful) guidance, also referred to as "new rules of engagement."[153] Of the four soldiers formally charged in this incident, two are serving eighteen-year sentences, while the others took plea bargains and/or received parole.[154] Colonel Steele, who consistently denied issuing the new rules of engagement, was given immunity from prosecution in exchange for his testimony against one of his soldiers.[155] The disparity in punishment calls into question the doctrine of command responsibility, which simply implies that leaders are accountable for the actions of their subordinates. An example of a case where an American commander was held responsible for the crimes of his subordinates is the trial of Henry Wirz, commander of Andersonville Prison in Georgia during the civil war in 1864. Of the 41,000 Union prisoners held in his facility, 12,000 died from abuse, murder, starvation, and disease. Wirz was subsequently found guilty of both omission and

---

[150] The practice of using nicknames to dehumanize the enemy and its culture still occurs informally within the U.S. military. The author has taken part in operational deployments between 2003 and 2007, where Iraqis and Afghans were called 'hajis,' with the caveat that "the hajis like being called by this nickname."

[151] Goldstein, et al, *The Peers Commission Report*, 9

[152] Stjepan Mestrovic, *Rules of Engagement? A Social Anatomy of an American War Crime: Operation Iron Triangle, Iraq* (New York: Algora Publishing, 2008), 21.

[153] Ibid., 113.

[154] The Associated Press, "Family: Soldier in Iraq Deaths Case Gets Parole," *Army Times* online (August 15, 2009) accessed March 1, 2012 http://www.armytimes.com/news/2009/08/ap_girouard_parole_081509/.

[155] Mestrovic, *Rules of Engagement?*, 23.

commission of war crimes—eighty-one years before the Geneva Conventions existed—and he was sentenced to death.[156]

The COIN principles that could have been implemented in the cases above come from chapter seven, "Leadership and Ethics for Counterinsurgency."[157] The opening points address the leader's responsibility to reconcile mission effectiveness, ethical standards, and thoughtful stewardship of the Nation's precious resources—human and material; the leader's responsibility to proactively establish and maintain the proper ethical climate of their organizations; and the leader's responsibility to respond quickly and aggressively to signs of illegal or unethical behavior.[158] Units with a stable ethical climate are likely to wage successful COIN campaigns that consist of a mix of offensive, defensive, and stability operations. In this type of environment, soldiers are prepared to conduct combat operations and nation building, sometimes simultaneously, which is why a healthy ethical climate and overall functionality of the unit must be intact before it enters the fight.

Key to understanding COIN, as compared with conventional military operations, is its nonmilitary, population-centric focus. Performing traditionally nonmilitary tasks in COIN requires knowledge of many diverse, complex subjects, including governance, economic development, public administration, and the rule of law.[159] The complexity of military operations can make progress in the COIN environment hard to measure, which is why commanders must adopt a decentralized approach and embrace a bottom-up learning model in order to defeat enemies and prevent civilian casualties.

This section described how harming civilians complicates an already complex operational environment, which is counterproductive to mission accomplishment. The vignette at the beginning of the chapter quoted the soldier who led the charge during a rape/murder incident indicating that he wanted to kill people. His sentiments surely do not represent the majority of the armed forces, but he is not the first to make such remarks. He and those involved clearly did not balance a reasonable

---

[156] Ibid., 163.
[157] Field Manual 3-24, *Counterinsurgency* (Washington, D.C.: Government Printing Office, 2006), 7-1.
[158] Ibid.
[159] Ibid., x.

sense of morality with the temptation to kill, nor were they provided necessary leader supervision which may have eliminated their ability to abandon their post in order to commit their crimes.

The balance of morality with killing was elevated to international political and military leaders with regard to bombing strategy and the moral debate surrounding the targeting of civilians during World War II. Furthermore, immediately following the bombing of Pearl Harbor, the political solution 'to prevent future attacks' was to incarcerate and interrogate U.S. citizens. The logic behind this pattern was revisited after the attacks of September 11, 2001. The psychological effects on the bomber pilots was not mentioned in this work, but the reality of the evolution from targeting military objectives to "enemy" civilians was felt by some, who obeyed the orders of their superiors anyway. Such was the case as the army underwent force transformation simultaneously as it became engaged in fighting two wars in the Middle East.

The consequences of a decade of ever-changing doctrine, multiple deployments, and the seemingly endless era of persistent conflict are still mostly unknown. The American public sees the media's interpretation of the war, and associated atrocities committed (enemy and friendly) in sound bites, but these condensed reports do not convey the complexities of daily operations in the theater of operations, nor do they portray the adjustment challenges of returning veterans not scheduled to deploy for yet another tour of duty. It is imperative that leaders take preventive measures to mitigate the risk associated with soldier reintegration as the military transitions back to its posts, camps, and stations, in an effort to posture for downsizing, budget constraints, and peacetime operations. The stress has taken its toll on the force and the output is predictable: lack of soldier restraint.

CONCLUSIONS

As the author completes this monograph, the incident involving an Army sergeant who killed sixteen civilians in the Kandahar Province of Afghanistan on March 11, 2012, added to the weight of the argument presented in this work. Media reports indicate that Staff Sergeant Robert Bales (on his fourth deployment since the start of the Global War on Terror) walked more than a mile from his base through three rural villages trying to break into homes, eventually getting into three separate homes where he killed and set fire to the inhabitants. Making matters worse, two other incidents, which offended local populations in Afghanistan (recent release of video footage of a group of marines urinating on dead militants and reports of a group of Army soldiers burning Korans), occurred shortly before the Kandahar killings. Reports say there is a "growing concern over a cascade of missteps and offenses that has cast doubt on the ability of NATO personnel to carry out their mission," which leaves "troops and trainers increasingly vulnerable to violence by Afghans seeking revenge."[160] Additionally (and predictably), condolences and apologies were offered to the Afghan president by the American president. This event elaborates this monograph's themes regarding the consequences of killing innocents: instant and ubiquitous media coverage and interpretation, political discourse involving questions about the efficacy of the American military in a COIN environment, and yet another tale of a service member who allegedly reached his breaking point as a result of the complexity of military operations.

The problem of military forces killing civilians (intentionally or inadvertently) is not new. History offers many examples, but this work focused on civilians killed by the U.S. military. This paper discussed events during and after World War II because the post-war evolution of the media, politics and international law, as well as the western way of war, shaped the way the public understands/justifies war and how the military fights today. When declaring victory after war, we must never glorify warfare itself; for it is the nature of combat that historically (and presently) brought misery and death to an untold number of civilians. Examples from World War II, the Vietnam War, as well as the recent conflicts in Iraq and Afghanistan reveal similarities, and possibly predictable patterns, that we must anticipate and prevent.

---

[160] Taimoor Shah and Graham Bowley, "U.S. Sergeant is Said to Kill 16 Civilians in Afghanistan," The New York Times online (March 11, 2012) accessed on March 15, 2012 at http://www.nytimes.com/2012/03/12/world/asia/afghanistan-civilians-killed-american-soldier-held.html?pagewanted=1&_r=1.

Using his own memories from World War II, veteran Edward W. Wood, Jr. explained his struggle to understand the nature of combat, the truth about atrocities committed by American soldiers, and his rejection of the glorification of war. World War II saw its fair share of atrocities from the unnecessary bombing of Royan, France by the United States,[161] and the rape line-ups where American soldiers stood in formation as women walked through scrutinizing each face in order to identify the one who raped her in the process of 'liberating' her town.[162] Throughout his book, he emphasized that war is—and always has been—about killing both enemy combatants *and* civilians. He argued that World War II 'improved' on the killing of innocents not only by mass exterminations on the ground, but also by killing from the air.[163] The resulting establishment of the Geneva Conventions and the United Nations regulated war and protected civilians from its danger. However, the media, since 1945, presented a "cleaned-up" version of World War II in newspapers, television, and movies, which effectively exonerated U.S. soldiers who committed atrocities during the war, and has served as the basis for the employment of the military by political leaders ever since.[164]

Investigations into the My Lai massacre, which occurred on March 16, 1968 (and kept secret for nearly four years[165]), uncovered trends found in modern examples of civilians killed during war. First, the U.S. military found itself, at least in part, fighting counterinsurgency/guerilla-style warfare where more than ninety percent of the American Division's combat injuries and deaths resulted from booby traps and land mines emplaced by an unseen enemy.[166] Second, there was a misunderstanding of, or blatant disregard for, the rules of engagement (which supposedly provided stringent restrictions on the use of firepower and called for clearance before firing on civilian areas), but ironically, some commanders treated brutalities such as rape, murder, and arson against the Vietnamese as petty and

---

[161] Wood, *Worshipping the Myths of World War II*, 96.
[162] Ibid., 150.
[163] Ibid., 21-22.
[164] Ibid., 5.
[165] Goldstein, et al., *The My Lai Massacre and Its Cover-up*, 2.
[166] Hersh, *Cover-Up*, 10.

rarely reported them.[167] The crux of the issue for the unit conducting attacks on their objectives

(Vietnamese villages) was the assumption that the intelligence regarding the nature of their enemy

target was accurate—and that killing everyone on the objective was approved at a higher level.

Furthermore, soldiers were expected to obey orders, particularly in combat, which means they would

destroy a village if they were so ordered. Third, in response to reports of prisoner mistreatment,

remedial training was directed in lieu of courts-martial.[168] Fourth, the investigation determined that

brigade commanders enabled permissive environments where atrocities were minimized or

ignored.[169]

In September of 2001 (thirty-three years after My Lai), the United States military found itself

preparing for the Global War on Terror. Examples of each of the four points mentioned above from

the Vietnam War occurred during our current war and are captured throughout this paper. There

exists a pattern in the combination of an unseen enemy in a counterinsurgency fight, the ambiguity of

the rules of engagement, prisoner abuse, and a permissive environment stemming from command

climate issues. The topic of civilian casualties is extraordinarily complex, which makes it difficult to

show systemic causality; however, the emergence of these patterns in many wars is clear. In our

current era, however, the media highlights these patterns, politicians apologetically explain them, and

the military obediently continues to fight. Yet even the most nuanced examination falls short of

explaining precisely why the U.S. military continues to harm foreign civilians.

Regardless of why it happens, the act of killing innocent civilians during war is

counterproductive to mission accomplishment and results in a decline in support for military

intervention forces.[170] This can have lasting effects on foreign policy. Reducing civilian casualties is a

moral and strategic issue, and should be analyzed separately from the other aspects of military

---

[167] Ibid., 34-35.
[168] Ibid., 41.
[169] Ibid., 252-253.
[170] The United States Institute of Peace, "Killing Friends, Making Enemies: The Impact and Avoidance of Civilian Casualties in Afghanistan," (July 2008),
http://www.usip.org/files/resources/USIP_0708_2.PDF.

operations. The following recommendations need consideration because these ideas may lessen the negative effects of war on civilians by taking a holistic, preventive approach, rather than treating symptoms of the problem after casualty events occur.

United Nations Security Council Resolution 1325 (UN 1325), passed in October of 2001, empirically linked gender equality, peace, and security together for the first time in history.[171] The UN peacekeeping and NATO implementation of UN 1325 indicate that security actors are more successful when peace and security missions, such as the protracted conflicts in Iraq and Afghanistan, include women in executing operations and decision-making. As a point of fact, none of the vignettes used in this monograph, nor any of the research used for historic context involving the killing of civilians during and since World War II, *ever* implicate women committing atrocities in *any* war. The United States does not currently have a national action plan for UN 1325 in place throughout its armed forces; however, the U.S. Marines have begun to utilize female engagement teams in Iraq and Afghanistan for targeted security activities. The U.S. government should develop a plan to operationalize UN 1325 across the Department of Defense.

When creating strategies involving the execution of urban operations among foreign civilian populations, many of whom are women, children, and the elderly, a mixed-gender planning team would prove beneficial. "[O]ver the long sweep of history, women have been, and will be, a pacifying force.[172] Furthermore, "women's presence makes male peacekeepers more reflective and responsible, and it broadens the skills and styles available within the mission, often with the effect of reducing

---

[171] Sahana Dharmapuri, "Just Add Women and Stir?" *Parameters*, vol. XLI, no. 1, (Spring 2011) 56-70. UN 1325 encompasses a range of complex issues such as judicial and legal reform, security sector reform, peace negotiations, peacekeeping, political participation, and protection from and response to sexual violence in armed conflict.
[172] Steven Pinker, *The Better Angels of Our Nature: Why Violence Has Declined* (New York: Viking, 2011), 527.

conflict and confrontation."[173] The United States military should implement UN 1325 prior to

becoming involved in its next combat mission in order to validate the aforementioned claims.

U.S. military operations and UN peacekeeping operations are steadily converging to such a

degree that the head of UN peacekeeping calls his forces serving in 118 countries, "the second largest

deployed army in the world."[174] Where American service members were once sent to defeat foreign

enemies, they are now also expected to maintain peace, establish conditions for political and

economic stability, and be advisors on matters of governance and security forces. They are also

organized to integrate with non-governmental organizations, and civilian agencies, in addition to

serving under a Foreign Service, or civilian chain of command. The U.S. government should conduct

a study based on the goal of streamlining nation-building efforts of the military and peacekeeping

missions of the UN under one command. Peacekeeping forces integrated with military intervention

forces may decrease incidences of violence against civilians.[175]

The use of anthropologists as cultural advisors is not a new practice. Called Human Terrain

Systems (HTS), members of these teams gather and disseminate information to military units on

indigenous, civilian cultures that live in the theater of war.[176] However, the HTS should expand to

include sociologists who study how the U.S. military could better integrate with foreign civilian

populations. Sociologists are experts in understanding what makes societies, such as military

organizations, successful, and what makes them dysfunctional. Sociologists are technically equipped

to advise commanders on how to maintain a functional command climate while his or her unit

develops a functioning coexistence with the foreign population for the duration of

---

[173] Vanessa Kent, "Protecting Civilians From UN Peacekeepers and Humanitarian Workers: Sexual Exploitation and Abuse," in Chiyuki Aoi, Et. Al., Eds., *Unintended Consequences of Peacekeeping Operations* (Tokyo: New York: Paris: United Nations University Press, 2007), 56.

[174] Joshua S. Goldstien, *Winning the War on War: The Decline of Armed Conflict Worldwide* (New York: Dutton, 2011), 309.

[176] George R. Lucas, Jr., *Anthropologists at Arms: The Ethics of Military Anthropology* (New York: Alta Mira Press, 2009), 81; See also Montgomery McFate and Steve Fondacaro, "Reflections on the Human Terrain System During the First 4 Years," *Prism* (online), Vol 2, No 4 (September 2011), accessed March 1, 2012 at http://www.ndu.edu/press/lib/images/prism2-4/Prism_63-82_McFate-Fondacaro.pdf.

combat/peacekeeping operations. Having an autonomous, trained expert in the field of sociology interact with a deployed unit would decrease the likelihood of a breakdown in the morale and discipline of a unit; and therefore lessen the likelihood of the commission of violent acts against local civilians.

Finally, a new approach to ethics training is necessary for the leadership of the U.S. military. Strategic and political failures have contributed to moral deficiencies among the officer corps.[177] Central to this breakdown is growing careerism, which is likely to increase in a budget-constrained environment, and can lead to risk aversion, cover-ups, avoidance of responsibility, and other behaviors that are counterproductive to mission accomplishment. Obtaining innovative ideas about how to improve ethics training from outside the armed forces may prevent further exacerbation of these issues, most of which were precursors to the commission of atrocities in several examples provided in this work.

---

[177] Richard H. Kohn, "Tarnished Brass: Is the U.S. Military Profession in Decline?" *World Affairs Journal* (Spring 2009), accessed March 5, 2012 at http://www.worldaffairsjournal.org/print/1253.

Bibliography

"6 Months for GI in Iraqi Drowning," CBS News, re-released February 11, 2009, accessed January 7, 2012 http://www.cbsnews.com/stories/2005/01/05/iraq/main664951.shtml.

"A Short History of NATO," posted online under NATO History, accessed February 20, 2012, http://www.nato.int/history/nato-history.html.

Adams, Cindy. "Hillary Clinton and Leon Panetta Condemn Marines Urinating on Taliban (video)," accessed January 13, 2012 http://www.examiner.com/us-headlines-in-national/hillary-clinton-and-leon-panetta-condemn-marines-urinating-on-taliban-video.

Adebjo, Adekeye and Chandra L. Sriram, eds. *Managing Armed Conflicts in the 21ˢᵗ Century*. London: Frank Cass Publishers, 2001.

Alia, Valerie. *Media Ethics and Social Change*. New York: Routledge, 2004.

Bacevich, Andrew, ed. *The Long War: A New History of U.S. National Security Policy Since World WarII*. New York: Columbia University Press, 2007.

Badescu, Cristina G. *"Humanitarian Intervention and the Responsibility to Protect: Security and Human Rights."* London and New York: Routledge, 2011.

Blanchard, Margaret A. *Revolutionary Sparks: Freedom of Expression in Modern America.* North Carolina: Oxford University Press, 1992.

Bourque, Stephen A., Ph.D. "Operational Fires: Lisieux and Saint Lo – The Destruction of Two Norman Towns on D-Day," *Canadian Military History*, vol. 19, no. 2 (Spring 2010).

Bowley, Graham and Matthew Rosenbert. "Video Inflames a Delicate Moment for U.S. in Afghanistan," The New York Times online (January 12, 2012), accessed January 13, 2012 http://www.nytimes.com/2012/01/13/world/asia/video-said-to-show-marines-urinating-on-taliban-corpses.html?pagewanted=1&_r=1.

Browder, Dewey. "Henry Morgenthau, Jr.: American Statesman and German American Jew," in Malcolm Muir, Jr., ed., *The Human Tradition in the World War II Era*. Wilmington, DE: Scholarly Resources Inc., 2001.

Carafano, James J. "Mastering the Art of Wiki: Understanding Social Networking and National Security," *Joint Force Quarterly*, Issue 60, 1ˢᵗ Quarter 2011, 73-78.

"Charter of the United Nations," *Handbook on the Peaceful Settlement of Disputes Between States*. New York: United Nations, 1992.

Clausewitz, Carl. *On War*. Princeton, New Jersey: Princeton University Press, 1976.

Coady, C.A.J. "Bombing and the Morality of War," in *Bombing Civilians: A Twentieth-Century History*. New York: London: The New York Press, 2009.

"Cover-up of Iraq Bridge Incident Admitted," USA Today, July 30, 2004, accessed January 7, 2012 http://www.usatoday.com/news/nation/2004-07-30-drowning-confession_x.htm.

Denton, Robert E., ed. *The Media and the Persian Gulf War*. Westport, CT: London: Praeger Publishers, 1993.

Dharmapuri, Sahana. "Just Add Women and Stir?" *Parameters*, vol. XLI, no. 1, (Spring 2011) 56-70.

"'Drowned Iraqi' Was Forced into River by Five U.S. Soldiers," (February 14, 2004) posted online at IslamWeb, The Independent, accessed March 19, 2012 at http://www.islamweb.net/ehajj/printarticle.php?id=57166&lang=E.

Dudney, Robert S. "Douhet," *AIR FORCE Magazine*, vol. 94, no. 4 (April 2011): 64-67, accessed December 3, 2011 http://www.airforce-magazine.com/MagazineArchive/Pages/2011/April%202011/0411douhet.aspx.

el-Nawawy, Mohammed, Ph.D. "Terrorist or Freedom Fighter?: The Arab Media Coverage of "Terrorism" or "So-Called Terrorism."" *Global Media Journal*, Vol 3, Issue 5, (Fall 2004) accessed February 10, 2012 http://lass.calumet.purdue.edu/cca/gmj/fa04/gmj-fa04-elnawawy.htm.

Engelhardt, Tom. "Going for Broke: Six Ways the AF-PAK War is Expanding," in Nick Turse, ed., *The Case for Withdrawal From Afghanistan*, London: New York: Verso, 2010.

Fallows, Deborah and Lee Rainie. "The Internet as a Unique News Source," Pew Internet and American Life Project, (July 8, 2004) accessed December 20, 2011, http://www.pewinternet.org/Reports/2004/Internet-as-Unique-News-Source/3-The-new-experience-of-war-images-online/1-Americans-are-turning-to-the-Internet-for-news-coverage-not-in-the-mainstream-news-media.aspx.

Field Manual 3-24, Counterinsurgency. Washington, D.C.: Government Printing Office, 2006.

Field Manual 7-0, Training for Full Spectrum Operations. Washington, D.C.: Government Printing Office, 2008.

Filkins, Dexter. "The Fall of the Warrior King," *The New York Times Magazine*, (October 23, 2005) accessed January 7, 2012 http://www.nytimes.com/2005/10/23/magazine/23sassaman.html?pagewanted=all.

Galal, Ashraf, et al. "The Image of the United States Portrayed in Arab Online World Journalism," available online at http://online.journalism.utexas.edu/2008/papers/GalalPaper.pdf, accessed December 10, 2011, p2. This paper was submitted for consideration to the Ninth International Symposium on Online Journalism at the University of Texas at Austin, April 4-5, 2008.

Geneva Conventions of August 12, 1949 For the Protection of War Victims. Department of State Publication 3938, General Foreign Policy Series 34, August 1950.

"Get Back From the Coast, Eisenhower Tells Europeans," *The Washington Post*, (June 6, 1944).

Glover, Jonathan. *Humanity: A Moral History of the Twentieth Century.* New Haven: London: Yale University Press, 2000.

Goldstein, Joshua S. *Winning the War on War.* New York: Penguin Group, 2011.

Goldstein, Joseph, Burke Marshall and Jack Schwartz. *The My Lai Massacre and Its Cover Up: Beyond the Reach of Law? The Peers Commission Report with a Supplement and Introductory Essay on the Limits of the Law.* New York: The Free Press, 1976.

Greenspan, Morris. *Soldier's Guide to the Laws of War.* Washington, D.C.: Public Affairs Press, 1969.

Guerilla Hunter Killer Smartbook: Tactics, Techniques, and Procedures. Accessed online March 1, 2012 http://info.publicintelligence.net/GuerrillaHunterKillerSmartbook.pdf.

Hakanen, Ernest A. and Alexander Nikolaev. *Leading to the 2003 Iraq War: The Global Media Debate.* Gordonsville, VA: Palgrave Macmillan, 2006.

Hammer, Joshua. "Death Squad," book review of *Black Hearts: One Platoon's Descent Into Madness in Iraq's Triangle of Death* by Jim Frederick, posted on The New York Times online, Sunday Book Review (March 11, 2010), accessed February 22, 2012, http://www.nytimes.com/2010/03/14/books/review/Hammer-t.html.

Hara, Thomas. "The Hara Family: The Story of a Nisei Couple," in Malcolm Muir, Jr., Ed., *The Human Tradition in the World War II Era.* Wilmington, DE: Scholarly Resources Inc., 2001.

Harriss, John, ed. *The Politics of Humanitarian Intervention.* London: Pinter Publishers, 1995.

Hersh, Seymour M. *Cover Up: The Army's Investigation of the Massacre at My Lai 4.* New York: Ramdom House, 1972.

_____. *My Lai-4: A Report on the Massacre and its Aftermath.* New York: Vintage, 1970.

Howard, Michael. "Reflections on the First World War" in Michael Howard (ed.), *Studies in War and Peace.* London, 1970.

Joint Publication 1-04, Legal Support to Military Operations. Washington D.C.: Government Printing Office, 2011.

Karpinski, Janis. *One Woman's Army: The Commanding General of Abu Ghraib Tells Her Story.* New York: Mirimax Books, 2005.

Kent, Vanessa. "Protecting Civilians From UN Peacekeepers and Humanitarian Workers: Sexual Exploitation and Abuse," in Chiyuki Aoi, et. al., eds., *Unintended Consequences of Peacekeeping Operations.* Tokyo: New York: Paris: United Nations University Press, 2007.

King, Tim. "Beheading Desecration Video of Dead U.S. Soldiers Released on Internet by Al Qaeda," Salem News online (July 11, 2006), accessed February 22, 2012 http://www.salem-news.com/articles/july112006/tucker_menchaca_71106.php.

Knell, Hermann. *To Destroy A City: Strategic Bombing and Its Human Consequences in World War II*, Cambridge: Da Capo Press, 2003.

Knickmeyer, Ellen. "In Haditha, Memories of a Massacre." The Washington Post online (May 27, 2006), accessed December 20, 2011 http://www.washingtonpost.com/wp-dyn/content/article/2006/05/26/AR2006052602069.html.

_____ . "Details Emerge in Alleged Army Rape, Killings," The Washington Post online (July 3, 2006) accessed February 20, 2012 http://www.washingtonpost.com/wpdyn/content/article/2006/07/02/AR2006070200673_pf.html.

Kohn, Richard H. "Tarnished Brass: Is the U.S. Military Profession in Decline?" *World Affairs Journal* (Spring 2009), accessed March 5, 2012 at http://www.worldaffairsjournal.org/print/1253.

Koppes, Clayton R. and Gregory D. Black. "What to Show the World: The Office of War Information and Hollywood, 1942-1945," *The Journal of American History*, Vol. 64, No. 1 (June 1977).

"Leaders Tackle Counterinsurgency and Civilian Casualties," (May 16, 2010) accessed December 20, 2011 http://www.isaf.nato.int/article/news/leaders-tackle-counterinsurgency-and-civilian-casualties.html.

Linder, Dough. "The Nuremburg Trials," accessed January 28, 2012 http://archives.un.org/ARMS/sites/ARMS/uploads/files/unwcc_finding_aid.pdf.

Lucas, Jr., George R. *Anthropologists at Arms: The Ethics of Military Anthropology*. New York: Alta Mira Press, 2009.

Martin, Randall. "A Brief History of Propaganda," in *Censored 2012: Sourcebook for the Media Revolution* by Mickey Huff and Project Censored. New York: Seven Stories Press, 2011.

Mayfield III., Thomas D. "A Commander's Strategy for Social Media," *Joint Force Quarterly*, Issue 60, 1st Quarter 2011, pp79-83.

McFate, Montgomery and Steve Fondacaro, "Reflections on the Human Terrain System During the First 4 Years," *Prism* (online), Vol 2, No 4 (September 2011), accessed March 1, 2012 at http://www.ndu.edu/press/lib/images/prism2-4/Prism_63-82_McFate-Fondacaro.pdf

McHale, Donald M. *"Hitler's Shadow War: The Holocaust and World War II."* New York: Copper Square Press, 2002.

Mestrovic, Stjepan G. *The Trials of Abu Ghraib: An Expert Witness Account of Shame and Honor.* Colorado: Paradigm Publishers, 2007.

_____ . *Postemotional Society.* London: Sage Publications, 1997.

_____ . *Rules of Engagement? A Social Anatomy of an American War Crime: Operation Iron Triangle, Iraq.* New York: Algora Publishing, 2008.

Miller, Paul. *Leadership in a Transnational World: The Challenge of Keeping the Peace.* Washington D.C.: The Institute for Foreign Policy Analysis, 2003.

Mogelson, Luke. "A Beast in the Heart of Every Fighting Man," The New York Times online, (April 27, 2011) accessed December 20, 2011 http://www.nytimes.com/2011/05/01/magazine/mag-01KillTeam-t.html?pagewanted=1&_r=2&ref=calvingibbs.

Muller, Eric L. *American Inquisition: The Hunt for Japanese American Disloyalty in World War II.* Chapel Hill: University of North Carolina Press, 2007.

Mulrine, Anna. "Pentagon Had Red Flags About Command Climate in 'Kill Team' Stryker Brigade," Christian Science Monitor online, accessed February 26, 2012 http://axcessnews.com/index.php/articles/show/id/21133.

Ng, Wendy. *Japanese American Internment During World War II: A History and Reference Guide.* Connecticut: London: Greenwood Press, 2002.

O'Hanlon, Michael E. *Expanding Global Military Capacity for Humanitarian Intervention.* Washington, D.C.: Brookings Institution Press, 2003.

Otero, L. M. "Army Sergeant Sentenced to Six Months," USA Today, January 8, 2005, accessed January 7, 2012 http://www.usatoday.com/news/world/iraq/2005-01-08-soldier-drowning_x.htm.

Pape, Robert A. *Bombing to Win: Air Power and Coercion in War.* Ithaca: London: Cornell University Press, 1996.

Paul, Christopher. *Reporters on the Battlefield: The Embedded Press System in Historical Context.* California: RAND, 2004.

Pelley, Scott. "Haditha Massacre Defendant: We Did What We Had To," CBS News online (January 6, 2012), accessed January 10, 2012 http://www.cbsnews.com/8301-18563_162-57354199/haditha-massacre-defendant-we-did-what-we-had-to/.

Pessen, Al. "Gates Apologizes for Afghan Civilian Deaths," Voice of America online (March 7, 2011), accessed January 21, 2012 http://www.voanews.com/english/news/asia/US-Defense-Secretary-Arrives-in-Kabul-Amid-Strained-Relations-117510188.html.

Pinker, Steven. *The Better Angels of Our Nature: Why Violence Has Declined.* New York: Viking, 2011.

"Reich Already Plans New War, Author Tells Legion Leaders," *The Washington Post*, (May 1, 1944).

Rice, Condoleeza. Memorandum to Senior Political and Military Leaders re: Declaratory Policy on Afghanistan (September 27, 2001), available online at Rumsfeld.com, accessed February 25, 2012, http://library.rumsfeld.com/doclib/sp/1502/2001-09-27%20from%20Condoleezza%20Rice%20re%20Declaratory%20Policy%20on%20Afghanistan-%20Memo%20Attachment.pdf.

Rubin, Alissa J. "Afghan Leader Calls Apology in Boys' Deaths Insufficient," The New York Times online (March 6, 2011), accessed January 21, 2012 http://www.nytimes.com/2011/03/07/world/asia/07afghanistan.html.

Rumsfeld, Donald. Memorandum to the President re: Strategic Thoughts (September 30, 2001), available online at Rumsfeld.com, accessed February 25, 2012

        http://library.rumsfeld.com/doclib/sp/272/2001-09-
        30%20to%20President%20Bush%20re%20Strategic%20Thoughts.pdf.

Shah, Saeed and Peter Beaumont. "US Drone Strikes in Pakistan Claiming Many Civilian Victims,"
        (July 17, 2011) accessed December 20, 2011
        http://www.guardian.co.uk/world/2011/jul/17/us-drone-strikes-pakistan-waziristan.

Shah, Taimoor and Graham Bowley. "U.S. Sergeant is Said to Kill 16 Civilians in Afghanistan," The
        New York Times online (March 11, 2012), accessed on March 15, 2012 at
        http://www.nytimes.com/2012/03/12/world/asia/afghanistan-civilians-killed-american-
        soldier-held.html?pagewanted=1&_r=1.

Shah Taimoor and Alissa J. Rubin. "Relatives Tell of Civilians Killed by U.S. Soldiers," The New
        York Times online (October 4, 2010), accessed December 20, 2011
        http://www.nytimes.com/2010/10/05/world/asia/05afghan.html?ref=calvingibbs.

Shriner, John F., Colonel U.S. Air Force. "Reflections on Douhet, The Classical Approach," *Air
        University Review* (January-February 1986), accessed December 3, 2011
        http://www.airpower.au.af.mil/airchronicles/aureview/1986/jan-feb/shiner.html.

"Single Atomic Bomb Shakes Japan With Force Mightier Than 20,000 Tons of TNT to Launch New
        Era of Power," *The Washington Post*, (August 7, 1945).

Sorley, Lewis. *A Better War: The Unexamined and Final Tragedy of America's Last Years in
        Vietnam*, Orlando: Harcourt Inc., 1999.

"Soldier Gets Life Sentence in Afghan Thrill-Killings," Fox News online (November 10, 2011),
        accessed January 15, 2012
        http://www.foxnews.com/us/2011/11/10/soldier-found-guilty-in-afghan-thrill-killings/.

Solis, Gary D. *Son Thang: An American War Crime.* New York: Bantam, 1997.

"Systemic Abuse of Afghan Prisoners," Human Rights Watch online (May 12, 2004), accessed
        February 21, 2012, http://www.hrw.org/news/2004/05/12/us-systemic-abuse-afghan-
        prisoners.

Tanaka, Yuki and Marilyn B. Young, eds. *Bombing Civilians, A Twentieth Century History,* (New
        York: The New Press, 2009.

"The Avalon Project: Documents in Law, History, and Diplomacy," posted on the Yale Law School
        Lillian Goldman Law Library website, accessed January 24, 2012
        http://avalon.law.yale.edu/subject_menus/lawwar.asp.

"The Geneva Conventions of 1949 and Their Additional Protocols," posted on the International
        Committee of the Red Cross (ICRC) website (October 29, 2010), accessed on January 24,
        2012 http://www.icrc.org/eng/war-and-law/treaties-customary-law/geneva-
        conventions/overview-geneva-conventions.htm.

"The International Afghanistan Conference Bonn 2011," posted on the United Nations Permanent
        Mission of Afghanistan to the United Nations in New York website (December 5, 2011)

accessed January 24, 2012 http://www.afghanistan-un.org/2011/12/the-international-afghanistan-conference-bonn-2011/.

The United States Institute of Peace, "Killing Friends, Making Enemies: The Impact and Avoidance of Civilian Casualties in Afghanistan," (July 2008) accessed December 3, 2011 http://www.usip.org/files/resources/USIP_0708_2.PDF.

The United States Strategic Bombing Survey. Washington, D.C.: Government Printing Office, 1945.

Tilghman, Andrew. "I Came Over Here Because I Wanted to Kill People," The Washington Post online (July 30, 2006), accessed February 20, 2012 http://www.washingtonpost.com/wp-dyn/content/article/2006/07/28/AR2006072801492.html.

Ucko, David H. *The New Counterinsurgency Era: Transforming the U.S. Military for Modern Wars.* Washington, D.C.: Georgetown University Press, 2009.

"U.S. Soldier: Drowning was Ordered," (July 28, 2004), posted on Aljazeera online, accessed March 19, 2012 at http://www.aljazeera.com/archive/2004/07/2008410102250891881.html.

Weiss, Thomas G. *Military-Civilian Interactions: Intervening in Humanitarian Crises.* New York: Oxford: Rowman and Littlefield Publishers, Inc., 1999.

Whitney, Craig R. *The Abu-Ghraib Investigations: The Official Reports of the Independent Panel and the Pentagon on the Shocking Prisoner Abuse in Iraq.* New York: Public Affairs, 2004.

Wolfowitz, Paul. Memorandum to Secretary Rumsfeld re: Use of Special Forces, (September 23, 2001), available online at Rumsfeld.com, accessed February 25, 2012, http://library.rumsfeld.com/doclib/sp/267/2001-09-23%20from%20Wolfowitz%20re%20Using%20Special%20Forces%20on%20Our%20Side%20of%20the%20Line.pdf.

Wood, Jr., Edward W. *Worshipping the Myths of World War II: Reflections on America's Dedication to War.* Washington, D.C.: Potomac Books, Inc., 2006.

www.ingramcontent.com/pod-product-compliance
Lightning Source LLC
Chambersburg PA
CBHW080545290526
45790CB00006B/2555